Guardians of Promise: Birthing the Promise Part 1

Njeri M. Pringle, Ed.D.

Cover art by LaDarryl Hollingsworth

@Copyright – 2021 – Njeri M. Pringle once copyright has been granted
Permission has been granted for various works and short quotations.
Scriptures taken from the Holy Bible, New International Version®, NIV®. Copyright © 1973, 1978, 1984, 2011 by Biblica, Inc.™ Used by permission of Zondervan. All rights reserved worldwide. www.zondervan.com The "NIV" and "New International Version" are trademarks registered in the United States Patent and Trademark Office by Biblica, Inc.™Scripture quotations marked (NIV) are taken from the Holy Bible, New International Version®, NIV®. Copyright © 1973, 1978, 1984, 2011 by Biblica, Inc.™ Used by permission of Zondervan. All rights reserved worldwide. www.zondervan.comThe "NIV" and "New International Version" are trademarks registered in the United States Patent and Trademark Office by Biblica, Inc.™ All Scripture quotations, unless otherwise indicated, are taken from the Holy Bible, New International Version®, NIV®. Copyright ©1973, 1978, 1984, 2011 by Biblica, Inc.™ Used by permission of Zondervan. All rights reserved worldwide. www.zondervan.comThe "NIV" and "New International Version" are trademarks registered in the United States Patent and Trademark Office by Biblica, Inc.™

All Scripture quotations, unless otherwise indicated, are taken from the Holy Bible, New International Reader's Version®, NIrV® Copyright © 1995, 1996, 1998, 2014 by Biblica, Inc.™ Used by permission of Zondervan. All rights reserved worldwide. www.zondervan.comThe "NIrV" and "New International Reader's Version" are trademarks registered in the United States Patent and Trademark Office by Biblica, Inc.™

All Scripture quotations, unless otherwise indicated, are taken from the Amplified Bible, Copyright © 2015 by The Lockman Foundation. Used by permission. Scripture taken from the New King James Version®. Copyright © 1982 by Thomas Nelson, Inc. Used by permission. All rights reserved.

Scripture quotations taken from the Amplified® Bible (AMP), Copyright © 2015 by The Lockman Foundation. Used by permission. www.lockman.org.

All material appearing on this Internet site is copyrighted © 2020 by Deuel Enterprises Inc., Gary, SD 57237 subject to the 1994 copyright notice, and by this additional proviso: Internet users are hereby granted permission to make printed and electronic copies of all matters appearing on this site so long as it is only for your personal use, and is not for sale or for any commercial purpose. Your copies must contain this notice: copyright © Deuel Enterprises, Inc. 1997 Gary, SD 57237. You are **not** hereby permitted to post an electronic copy on the World Wide Web or any other place where it can be accessed by other people, but you can post a link to this site wherever desired.

Scripture quotations marked HCSB are taken from the Holman Christian Standard Bible®, Used by Permission HCSB ©1999,2000,2002,2003,2009 Holman Bible Publishers. Holman Christian Standard Bible®, Holman CSB®, and HCSB® are federally registered trademarks of Holman Bible Publishers.

Copyright © 2021 Njeri M. Pringle

All rights reserved.

ISBN: 979-8-9852799-0-0

Guardians of Promises: Birthing the Promise (Part 1)

DEDICATION

Dear God,

Breathe your word and heart on these pages. Through the writing of these books teach me about the Promise Keeper and build my trust not on the promises but on the character of the Promise Maker. Lord, help me be ignited as a promise pursuer and help these words ignite others along with me to become promise possessors or possessors of the "more than promised."

In Jesus' name
Your daughter, bride, promise pursuer
Njeri Pringle

Daniel 11:32 **(Amplified Bible)** "And such as do wickedly against the covenant shall he corrupted by flatteries: **but the people that do <u>know</u> their God shall be <u>strong,</u> and <u>do exploits.</u>**

FOREWORDS

This book is inspired, fresh, and engaging. It invites the reader on a disciplined journey. Although the promises are for everyone, they mean something different for each of us. Even if we are promised the destination, we are all starting the journey from different baselines. There are exercises throughout the book for readers who need a hands-on approach; there are reflections for the more meditative readers; there are citations for the skeptics: it is a complete map to go on a promise hunt.

Promises, like redemption, are freely given. Receiving, however, is the difficult part. There is nothing to earn; but how would we walk, talk, interact, engage, and love if we were truly and deeply filled with the Lord's promises? What would our lives and our hearts look like and feel like if we truly knew what our Father wants for us? This book is full of hope. It offers a practical approach to a generous topic. The rigor and the humility of the writer is inviting the reader to have reflection and introspection to make place for the true blessings that our Lord promised us.

Minister Vivian Vaughan

CONTENTS

	Acknowledgments	i
1	Chapter 1 – Stages of Promise Development	2
2	Chapter 2 – What is a Promise?	5
3	Chapter 3 – 1st Promises	6
4	Chapter 4 – Rainbow Promise	8
5	Chapter 5 – Detour	10
6	Chapter 6 – Who's Going to the Promise Land with You?	12
7	Chapter 7 – Major Promise	13
8	Chapter 8 – Reward & Protection	14
9	Chapter 9- Gestation: Promised Land (Covenant)	21
10	Chapter 10 – Subverting God's Way	22
11	Chapter 11 – Hagar Leaves	27
12	Chapter 12 – Secondary Promises & Counterfeits	30
13	Chapter 13 – Name & Nature Change	32
14	Chapter 14 – The Blessing, Promise, Covenant with God	36
15	Chapter 15 – Distinguishing those Set Aside for the Promise	39
16	Chapter 16 – Circumcised Heart vs. Uncircumcised Heart	44
17	Chapter 17 – A Name Change for Sari	46
18	Chapter 18 – Becoming	50
19	Chapter 19 – Too Good to Be True	52
20	Chapter 20 – Old Friends vs. New Name & Nature	54
21	Chapter 21 – Secondary or Inferior Promise	56
22	Chapter 22 – Obedience and Honor to Covenant	58

23	Chapter 23 – Hospitality: An Offering of Grace	60
24	Chapter 24 – Angelic Visitation	62
25	Chapter 25 – Proclamation of the Promise: Gifts Make Room	64
26	Chapter 26 – Our Laughter	66
27	Chapter 27 – Truth Over Lies	68
28	Chapter 28 – Can God Trust Us Enough to Tell Us or Show Us His Plans for Us?	69
29	Chapter 29 – Intimacy & Obedience Fosters Trust	71
30	Chapter 30 – God Judges Sin but Shows Mercy: Intercession	74
31	Chapter 31 – God's Protection and Favor	78
32	Chapter 32 – Submission: Mind over Matter	81
33	Chapter 33 – Looking Back & Treasures in Heaven	84
34	Chapter 34 – God's Continued Protection	87
35	Chapter 35 – Intercession, Protection, & Integrity	90
36	Chapter 36 – Blessings in Obedience	94
37	Chapter 37 – Getting Rid of the Counterfeits (Inferior Promises)	98
38	Chapter 38 – The Weight and Cost to Carry Counterfeits	100
39	Chapter 39 – Mourning of the Perceived Death of the Promise	101
40	Chapter 40 – But God Hears	104
41	Chapter 41 – Conclusion	106

ACKNOWLEDGMENTS

All honor to my Heavenly Father, the ultimate Promise Giver & Keeper.

INTRODUCTION

The pains of regret are often felt when it is too late for recovery. Too late, to fully take advantage of opportunities missed. Too late, to say I am sorry or more importantly I love you. The pains of regret are often realized in hindsight. A life fully lived has few regrets. A cautiously lived life with everything in its place, rarely is the life that sparks revolution in oneself or others. At the end of this life, will I have lived fully or packed my life full of (things, people, places but not purpose).

This book is a journey that parallels our collective and solitary walks of life. We are all created alike from a seed but few of us really know that we carry seeds of promise. The seeds of promise that can change our lives and the lives of others. If we fail to recognize that we are seed carriers we will fail to protect and nurture the promise. Most often we miscarry or abort the seeds of promise because they come at great cost (mainly submission: we must submit our plans to the Promise Maker and Promise Keeper). If we fail to submit our seeds of promise back to God, they mutate into a parasitic organism that will suck the life, hope, and purpose out of us. We create counterfeits. To rediscover your seeds of promise, join me on a journey to better understanding the Promise Giver and Keeper.

Prayer

> Lord, please breathe on our time and commitment throughout this study. Let your word and your presence transform us more into the image of the Promise Giver and Keeper. Let us become more like you, so that we may receive your power to fulfill your commission in Jesus' name amen. Feel free to add to this prayer point:
>
> _____
> _____
> _____
> _____

Disclaimer: Please note that as you embark on this study that I have chosen the translation of scripture which best amplifies the concepts. Please use the translation that work best for your understanding.

CHAPTER 1: STAGES OF PROMISE DEVELOPMENT

The journey of the *Guardians of Promise* began with a clear directive from God and a hesitant but obedient response from me. The details of the conversation are unclear; however, it was a directive to write about promises. I vowed, Lord, if you wake me up "I will not negotiate." We all know what negotiation translates into, a compromise that is not really a compromise as we are striving to "get our way." However, this conversation and my stance were different. I told God, I will not tell You how little sleep I have had, I will not tell You about my early morning or all-day commitments. I will rise, I will read, and I will write.

The process began with God nudging me out of bed at 3am or a little after. Early in the process, I researched promises. I tested out titles such as: "Guardians of Promise, Knowing the Promise Keeper, The Keeper of the Promises, and the Pursuit of the Promise." However, the "Guardians of the Promise" moved my heart, it spoke of ways in which we can protect the promise. I envisioned a treasure box illuminating light while being guarded by two angels with expanded wings. I could not see either of their forms, just one of each of their wings meeting in the center to cover and protect the treasure box.

Quickly, I thought how each of us, have hidden treasures in us: **2 Corinthians 4:7 (KJV)** 7 But we have this treasure in earthen vessels, that the excellency of the power may be of God, and not of us.

My first day was spent examining the treasure, by asking God for guiding questions:
1. What were some of the first promises?
2. Who made the first promise, when, why, and to whom?
3. The processing of Promise:
    a. Thought(conception) of the Promise
    b. Proclamation of the Promise
    c. Acknowledgement of the Promise
    d. Making, Accepting, Rejecting, or negotiating the Promise
    e. Sabotage of the Promise
    f. Pursuing, Receiving, or Possessing the Promise

I knew much like physical conception, promise conception had all the same tenets. The tenets of promise conception include intimacy, fertilization, implantation, gestation and development, labor (pain), and delivery which are the same for either a baby or a promise. Thus, if the promise can be birthed it could also be miscarried or aborted. How do we carry the promise to term? How can we give birth to more than just wind (nothingness)? **Isaiah 26:18 (NIV)** We were with child, we writhed in labor, but we gave birth to wind. We have not brought salvation to the earth, and the people of the world have not come to life. The Guardians of Promise will be organized with the following segments: intimacy, conceptualization, gestation, labor, and delivery.

Intimacy

Intimacy is the process by which we discover the Character of the Promise Giver and Keeper and the posture of the promise receiver (us). Through intimacy we come to know our identity as branches (Seed Carriers) connected to the vine. We also know that when disconnected from the vine the Seeds of Promises SOPs; become mutations or counterfeits.

Conceptualization

Conceptualization is the process in which we come to recognize the SOP and our role as seed carriers. The conception phase of the promise process is the time in which we must fully accept the authentic seed of promise in God's will and way but if God's way is circumvented, we conceive a counterfeit. The conception phase is also the phase in which we are most vulnerable to miscarry or abort the SOP, thus, identity birthed from intimacy helps root us and the seeds of promise.

Gestation

We enter the gestation phase when we have accepted the responsibility to carry, protect, and give birth to the SOP. The responsibility is great, and so is the understanding that we will face obstacles and challenges. In facing obstacles and challenges we are forced to be transformed into the images that God sees when He sees us.

Labor

We entered labor when we start to experience the pressure of being Seed Carriers; the pressure to deliver is great. Often, this is the time in which, much like Moses the enemy is trying to destroy the SOP before birth. The pressure or pain during this period is great, and we often fear destruction. But this is the time to endure. Much like David, we must remind ourselves of the character of the Promise Giver (God) and His faithfulness.

Delivery

Delivery is when we are successful in carrying, protecting, and birthing the Seeds of Promise. Often, the pain is forgotten in the light of beauty of the fulfillment of God's promises. Delivery is the phase in which we can give God praise and rejoice in His faithfulness. We must be careful to remember this delivery or deliverance as it galvanizes us to continue to give birth to more SOPs.

The phases of promise conception to delivery or deliverance are not as linear as we would like to believe. As intimacy is needed throughout each stage or phase, as we have seen the need for intimacy: when seeking confirmation in conceptualization, maintaining the faith during gestation, and finding strength during labor and delivery. Thinking points and questions:

> What stages of promise conception are you currently in? What are the characteristics of this phase?
>
> _____
> _____
> _____
> _____

Prayer:

> Lord, no matter the phase we are in, You are the same God **Hebrews 13:8 (NIV)**. Let's us rest in this truth! In Jesus' name, amen.

Intimacy & Conceptualization

Intimacy is the process by which we discover the Character of the Promise Giver and Keeper and the posture of the promise receiver (us). Through intimacy we come to know our identity as branches (Seeds of Carriers) connected to the vine. We also know that when disconnected from the vine the Seeds of Promises (SOPs) become mutations or counterfeits.

Conceptualization is the process by which we come to recognize the SOP and our role as seed carriers. The conception phase of the promise process is the time in which we must fully accept the authentic seed of promise (God's will and way) or if God's way is circumvented, we conceive a counterfeit. The conception phase is also the phase in which we are most vulnerable to miscarry or abort the SOP, thus, identity birthed from intimacy helps root us and the seeds of promise.

CHAPTER 2: WHAT IS A PROMISE?

What is a promise, and how is it established? Does the Promise Maker's character bear on the credibility of the promise? I thought, well, I can surely get the definition of a promise; I made promises countless times. Others have also made promises to me. I have both kept and broken many of my promises to myself, others, and especially God. Remember earlier when we were talking about negotiating? Well, when we are in trouble, we make extensive promises to God. If You just deliver me from this situation, I (fill in the blank). Either we tell God the things that we will or will not do, should He see fit to rescue us again. What is a promise, and is it dependent upon the character of the promise maker? If so, there is no permanent assurance on my side of the promise fulfillment, as circumstances may prevent me from keeping a promise. However, there is an assurance of promise fulfillment with God (the Promise Maker and Keeper)! **Numbers 23:19 (KJV).**

In defining promise, the word covenant appeared; thus, my research took a turn to discover the first covenant: what parties were involved, was it fulfilled, what was the character of the Promise Maker, and the posture of the promise receiver? Covenants and promises are also considered to be declarations **Job 22:28 (KJV)** Thou shalt also decree a thing, and it shall be established. I am beginning to understand that promises have power when they are professed.

Thinking point and Question:

    What are you professing over your life, your promises, your relationships, etc.?

_____

_____

Prayer:

    Lord, help us to stand firm on the faithfulness of Your word and character. Let us be steadfast in our professions of faith, as well as our word and promises to You, ourselves, and others. Let us honor You by also honoring Your and our word in Jesus' name, amen. Feel free to add to this prayer point:

_____

_____

CHAPTER 3: 1ST PROMISES
Dominion: Law, Command, or Promise

Genesis 1:26 (KJV) And God said, let us make man in our image, after our likeness; and let them have dominion over the fish and the sea, and over the fowl of the air, and over the cattle, and over the all the earth, and over every creeping thing that creepeth upon the earth.

1st Thinking Point and Question:

> Was there a promise within this law, command, a promised-them (plural form meaning) more than one, more than Adam? Man and female were created in Adam. Promises contained within the command lead me to think that the posture of the recipient is just as important as the command or promise. Obedience will be a factor in the fulfillment of this command. Is God calling you to multiply something today that seems like an impossible command? If so, what is a reasonable response? Where will you get help to empower you to complete this task(s)?

_____

_____

_____

_____

2nd Thinking Point:

> The concept of Eve containment within Adam is a foreshadowing of the trinity. God's command to Adam to multiply; is a revelation that we are made in the image of God (Father, Son Jesus, and the Holy Spirit) as we have spirit, soul, and flesh. How is your understanding of God impacting the way you see yourself in His image?

_____

_____

_____

_____

Genesis 6:18 (NIV) -Some one of the first covenants and or promises of God were of salvation from destruction.

Genesis 8:11 **(NIV)** - The dove is a foreshadowing of a greater promise and greater salvation

Genesis 8:21 **(NIV)** - God promises not to destroy everything by water.

Genesis 8:22 **(NIV)** - Permanency of God's promises - Night and day will not cease.

Genesis 9:9 **(NIV)** - God's covenant and generational blessings

Genesis 9: 3 **(NIV)** - Promise of meat (provision)

    Given you all things (past tense)

Questions:

    What are the things that have been given to you and me?

_____

_____

_____

_____

    How can we steward them well? I believe God gave me the Guardians of Promise and I have been asking Him how to steward these books well?

_____

_____

_____

_____

Prayer:

    Lord, teach us how to steward our giftings and Your anointing well. More importantly, Lord, help us never to take for granted You and Your presence as the greatest of these gifts. Lord, help us not become complacent or apathetic to Your invitations to spend time with You or to serve You by serving others. Lord, we ask and submit our giftings back under Your submission and Lordship; we will not use our gifts for self-seeking fame. We want to make You famous; we want Your name to be glorified and magnified in all of the earth. In Jesus' name, amen.

CHAPTER 4: RAINBOW PROMISE
<u>God's Symbol of Promise & Covenant</u>

Genesis 9:11-17 (AMPC) I will establish my covenant or pledge with you: never again shall all flesh be cut off by the waters of a flood; neither shall there ever again be a flood to destroy the earth and make it corrupt.12: And God said, this is the token of the covenant (solemn pledge) which I am making between me and you and every living creature that is with you, for all future generations:13:I set my bow [rainbow] in the cloud, and it shall be a token or sign of a covenant or solemn pledge between Me and the earth.14: And it shall be that when I bring clouds over the earth and the bow [rainbow] is seen in the clouds,15: I will [earnestly] remember my covenant or solemn pledge which is between me and you and every living creature of all flesh; and the waters will no more become a flood to destroy and make all flesh corrupt.16: When the bow [rainbow] is in the clouds and I look upon it, I will [earnestly] remember the everlasting covenant or pledge between God and every living creature of all flesh that is upon the earth. 17: And God said to Noah, this [rainbow] is the token or sign of the covenant or solemn pledge which I have established between Me and all flesh upon the earth.

The rainbow serves as a token of God's promise and a symbol of promises. As I was moving through Exodus, I remembered one morning (it was a challenging morning). I knew that it was raining, and I happened to look out to the driver's side mirror and notice rainbow(s) in the sky. At that time, I made declarations that I would become a promise pursuer. I want all that God has for me! I settled something in my heart that would later unfold through the process of writing this book. That day, I started to trust God as the Giver of the promise; that day, I started believing that (my then-current) circumstances were not an indication that God had forgotten His promises to me. More importantly, I had not disqualified myself from the promise due to some action and or inaction. I was reminded that God is a God of covenant. He does not lie, He stands by His word, and so those things that were promised will be fulfilled.

Question

Normally, when I am in fearful situations, like a plane ride or such; normally I calm my fears by reminding God that I cannot leave until the fulfillment of the promises. What are your reminder-promises?

_____
_____
_____
_____

Prayer

Lord, although the fulfillment of promise may be a reminder of Your faithfulness. Let us see Your presence and Your love as our anchor, anchor us in Your love and joy **Psalm 16:11 (NIV)**. Let Your presence anchor us in our identities as joint heirs with Christ. Let Your presence remind us in Jesus' name, amen. Feel free to add to this prayer point:

_____
_____
_____
_____

Notes & Overall discoveries:

CHAPTER 5: DETOUR

3rd Party Blessings or Promises: Noah to His Sons

Genesis 9:26-27 (NIV)

Genesis 9:28-29 (NIV)

Promise of enlargement as a nation

Genesis 12:1-3 (NIV)

Genesis 12:7 (NIV)

One of the first promises fulfilled, despite man's detour, happened when Abram went down into Egypt and lied about his marriage (to Sarai) to pharaoh. However, despite the lie, God blessed Abram. Thus, the promise was fulfilled despite the detour to Egypt and the character flaw (lying).

Genesis 12: 16-20 (AMPC): And he treated Abram well for her sake; he acquired sheep, oxen, he-donkeys, menservants, maidservants, she-donkeys, and camels. 17: But the Lord scourged Pharaoh and his household with serious plagues because of Sarai, Abram's wife. 18: And Pharaoh called Abram and said, what is this that you have done to me? Why did you not tell me that she was your wife? 19: Why did you say, she is my sister, so that I took her to be my wife? Now then, here is your wife; take her and get away [from here]! 20: And Pharaoh commanded his men concerning him, and they brought him on his way with his wife and all that he had.

Genesis 13: 2 (AMPC): And Abraham was very rich in cattle; in silver, and in gold.

Questions

> Abraham left his wilderness wealthy and enriched physically. However, do we know if his character had been altered by the experience in the wilderness?

_____

_____

_____

_____

How have you left places of bondage-Egypt? Were you enlarged, materially or otherwise? Were there alterations to your character?

_____
_____
_____
_____

Were some of your "Egypt" experiences detours or were you instructed to go to Egypt by God? This may vary based upon your experiences. Did it take a while to recover if they were detours? For Abram, He almost lost his wife. What did you lose or almost lose because of your Egypt experience?

_____
_____
_____
_____

Prayer:

Lord, help us to seek You whether we are in a God-prescribed wilderness or one of our own makings. Lord, let our hearts be calibrated back to You. Let us not focus on the fear of pain of losing as sometimes to lose is to gain. In Jesus' name, amen. Feel free to add to this prayer point:

_____
_____
_____
_____

Notes & Overall Discoveries:

CHAPTER 6: WHO'S GOING TO THE PROMISE LAND WITH YOU?

<u>Are You Walking Alone?</u>

<u>Genesis 13:1-11</u> (NIV)

Along this journey of becoming promise pursuers, we often must leave things, attitudes, attributes, and sometimes people behind. We cannot take everyone into the "Promised Land." Abram's experience with Lot is an example of when our values differ from others, more specifically when our walks of obedience to the voice of God are different. Indeed, a time when we must separate as two can only walk together if they are in agreement. Nevertheless, this does not mean that we will never walk the same road again; however, it is the will of the Father Who determines if our roads converge.

The promise will remain the promise no matter how many people come and go. The promise will remain the promise even if only you hear and understand what the Promise Maker is instructing you to do. Obedience will lead to greater ability to hear and heed the instructions of the Father, thus, posturing us to see the fulfillment of the promise. **<u>Genesis 13:12-15</u> (AMPC)**: 12 Abram dwelt in the land of Canaan, and Lot dwelt in the cities of the [Jordan] Valley and moved his tent as far as Sodom and dwelt there.13 But the men of Sodom were wicked and exceedingly great sinners against the Lord. 14 The Lord said to Abram after Lot had left him, Lift up now your eyes and look from the place where you are, northward and southward and eastward and westward; 15 For all the land which you see I will give to you and to your posterity forever.

Question:

> Who are your "Lots"? What have you already given up or will give up to maintain your relationships with your Lot? How is maintaining this relationship impacting your promise fulfillment?

_____

_____

_____

_____

Prayer:

Lord, please let us release and let go of everyone and everything that will hinder promise fulfillment in Jesus' name. Help us to properly mourn relationships and people that we have been released from, while also seeking Your heart on the matters of reconciliation. Feel free to add to this prayer:

_____

_____

_____

_____

Notes & Overall Discoveries:

CHAPTER 7: MAJOR PROMISE

Create Nations from Your Seed

Genesis 13:16-18 (AMPC) And I will make your descendants like the dust of the earth, so that if a man could count the dust of the earth, then could your descendants also be counted. 17 Arise, walk through the land, the length of it and the breadth of it, for I will give it to you. 18 Then Abram moved his tent and came and dwelt among the oaks or terebinths of Mamre, which are at Hebron, and built there an altar to the Lord.

Questions:

What has God promised you?

_____
_____
_____
_____

As He told Abram "Arise, walk through the land," what instructions has God given you?

_____
_____
_____
_____

Prayer & declaration: Lord, we remove any idols including ourselves and the promises off the altars of our hearts. We build altars to You alone God, we praise You for Your goodness. We will practice gratitude as a form of worship in Jesus' name, amen. This will be a good day to pray against any forms of idolatry, feel free to put your prayer points here:

_____
_____
_____
_____

CHAPTER 8: REWARD & PROTECTION

Genesis 15:1 (AMPC) After these things, the word of the Lord came to Abram in a vision, saying, Fear not, Abram, I am your Shield, your abundant compensation, and your reward shall be exceedingly great.

Questions:

> When examining this vision, the questions that come are the how(s), why(s), when(s): how will you bless me or fulfill this promise? What are your: how, why, when questions? How, if any, does asking these questions change your posture toward the Promise Maker and your possible response to His instruction?

_____

_____

_____

_____

> God is so faithful to answer the how(s) sometime; however, sometimes he may not tell us the whys or even when(s) or vice versa. He may tell us the why(s) but not the how(s) and when(s). If all was uncovered this would not be a faith walk but a see walk.

2 Corinthians 5:7 (NKJV) 7 For we walk by faith, not by sight.

God's answer:

> **Genesis 15:2-6 (AMPC):** 2 And Abram said, Lord God, what can You give me, since I am going on [from this world] childless and he who shall be the owner and heir of my house is this [steward] Eliezer of Damascus? 3 And Abram continued, look, you have given me no child; and [a servant] born in my house is my heir. 4 And behold, the word of the Lord came to him, saying, <u>this man shall not be your heir, but he who shall come from your own body shall be your heir. 5 And He brought him outside [his tent into the starlight] and said, look now toward the heavens and count the stars—if you are able to number them. Then He said to him, so shall your descendants be.</u>

Abram's response: **Genesis 15:6 (AMPC)** And he [Abram] believed in (trusted in, relied on, remained steadfast to) the Lord, and He counted it to him as righteousness (right standing with God).

I believe that Abram's response is the response of submission and trust; this posture sets us up to experience the blessings and miracles of God.

Genesis 15: 7 (AMPC) And He said to him, I am the [same] Lord, who brought you out of Ur of the Chaldees to give you this land as an inheritance.

Question:

> What is your inheritance?
>
> _____
> _____
> _____
> _____

Please read the story of the Prodigal Son **Luke 15:11-32 (AMPC).** The question of inheritance is one that I have been asking God – likened to the prodigal son's brother who was faithful with work (but maybe his heart and his motives were not right). Is the heart motives the seat for reaping and sowing? Does purity of purpose drive the law of reaping and sowing? Do corrupt motives hinder or produce a different type of undesirable harvest? How can we avoid this place of bitterness and barrenness? Because although the brother was active, his actions did not produce the desired effect.

Questions:

> In searching your heart, how do you distinguish between pure and impure motives?
>
> _____
> _____
> _____
> _____

> Do you think that promise fulfillment is contingent upon the posture of the promise receiver? If so, what is your posture concerning some unfulfilled promises?

_____
_____
_____
_____

Is all barrenness a condition of the heart? If so, how can we reverse the state of barrenness?

_____
_____
_____
_____

Abram's Question: **Genesis 15:8 (AMPC)** But he [Abram] said, Lord God, by what shall I know that I shall inherit it?

God's Answer:

Genesis 15:9-16 (AMPC) And He said to him, Bring to Me a heifer three years old, a she-goat three years old, a ram three years old, a turtledove, and a young pigeon.10 And he brought Him all these and cut them down the middle [into halves] and laid each half opposite the other; but the birds he did not divide.11 And when the birds of prey swooped down upon the carcasses, Abram drove them away.12 When the sun was setting, a deep sleep overcame Abram, and a horror (a terror, a shuddering fear) of great darkness assailed and oppressed him.13 And [God] said to Abram, know positively that your descendants will be strangers dwelling as temporary residents in a land that is not theirs [Egypt], and they will be slaves there and will be afflicted and oppressed for 400 years. [Fulfilled in Exod. 12:40.]14 But I will bring judgment on that nation whom they will serve, and afterward they will come out with great possessions.15 And you shall go to your fathers in peace; you shall be buried at a good old (hoary) age. 16 And in the fourth generation they [your descendants] shall come back here [to Canaan] again, for the iniquity of the Amorites is not yet full and complete.

God told Abram amazing things --the prophecy including the blessings and hardships that were to come. God promised Abram riches, long life, and peace for him personally. God also promised Abram, that his descendants would endure captivity and oppression; however, he would punish their oppressors and grant them deliverance. Abram received a generational blessing from God. In examining generational blessings, we see that God is faithful to His word. He remembers His words in times of disobedience. He remembers His word in times of unfaithfulness from His children. HE REMEMBERS AND KEEPS HIS WORD!

Questions

    Has God given you or your family a generational blessing?

_____

_____

_____

_____

    How have you been mandated to carry those generational blessings?

_____

_____

_____

_____

Prayer:

    Lord, we honor You and are honored by You that You have granted us generational blessings, please help us to follow the mandates in which to carry these mantles in Jesus' name, amen. Please feel free to add to this prayer:

_____

_____

_____

_____

Notes & Overall Discoveries:

Gestation

We enter the gestation phase when we have accepted the responsibility to carry, protect, and give birth to the SOP. The responsibility is great, and so is the understanding that we face obstacles and challenges. In facing obstacles and challenges we are forced to be transformed into the images that God sees when He sees us.

CHAPTER 9: PROMISED LAND (COVENANT)

<u>Covenant</u>

Genesis 15:18-21 (AMPC): 18 On the same day the Lord made a covenant (promise, pledge) with Abram, saying, To your descendants I have given this land, from the river of Egypt to the great river Euphrates—the land of 19 The Kenites, the Kenizzites, the Kadmonites,20 The Hittites, the Perizzites, the Rephaim,21 The Amorites, the Canaanites, the Girgashites, and the Jebusites.

I thought it was amazing that God spoke of the Promised land but also the obstacles and or enemies that Israel would have to defeat in order to obtain the promise. There is no Promise Land without the "ites" without the enemies and or obstacles of promise.

Questions:

What "ites" have your encountered on your way to promise fulfillment?

_____
_____
_____
_____

Have you defeated some "ites"? If so, which ones? If not, has God given you a plan on how to defeat the ites?

_____
_____
_____
_____

Some "ites" that I have encountered while writing this book are fear and procrastination, as this book was written in 2015 and is now being published in 2022. Having a God devised plan eliminates the unnecessary delays.

Prayer:

Lord, we thank you that You are faithful to reveal both the promises and the obstacles. Lord, please help us to seek out your instruction on how to defeat the "ites". If the "ite" is fear, please help us to unroot lies that make us look like grasshoppers in our own eyes **Numbers 13:33 (NIV)**. As we know, that if we fear, procrastination is not far behind. Give us strategy to be fearless and conquer our giants in the name of Jesus, amen. Feel free to add to this prayer point:

_____

_____

_____

_____

Notes & Overall Discoveries:

CHAPTER 10: SUBVERTING GOD'S WAY

<u>Taking Matters into Our Own Hands – Assigning Blame to God's Character</u>
"Misinterpretation of the Promise or Instruction of How to Obtain the Promise.
Genesis 16:1-4 (AMP): Now Sarai, Abram's wife, had borne him no children. She had an Egyptian maid whose name was Hagar.2 And Sarai said to Abram, see here, the Lord has restrained me from bearing [children]. I am asking you to have intercourse with my maid; it may be that I can obtain children by her. And Abram listened to and heeded what Sarai said.3 So Sarai, Abram's wife, took Hagar her Egyptian maid, after Abram had dwelt ten years in the land of Canaan, and gave her to her husband Abram to be his [secondary] wife.4 And he had intercourse with Hagar, and she became pregnant; and when she saw that she was with child, she looked with contempt upon her mistress and despised her.

The attitude of obedience is important when waiting for the promise to be fulfilled, and it speaks more of our character than God's. What makes us untrustworthy of the promise? Often, God is working out the kinks in our character because the obtainment of the promise could be to our detriment. The obtainment of the promise could actually become death to purpose. The purpose of the promise always has Kingdom intent, such as salvation, healing, and deliverance. Promise obtainment should never make the pursuer to lose purpose, peace, salvation, healing or deliverance. If so, we can trace if the promise was still under God's control or preview. If it is under God's control, even in struggle there should be peace. If the promise is still under God's mandate and way of completion, the evidence will produce and enlarge the Kingdom of God, not the Kingdom of Self.

Doing it our way is a rejection of the "promise" and promotion of Kingdom purposes and more aligned with selfishness (failure to submit our will for His). Doing it our way also serves as rejecting God's provision, protection, and means of fulfillment of promise or enlargement of His Kingdom.

Question:

    Is the promise still under God's control? If not, how can we resubmit it back to Him?

_____

_____

_____

_____

Prayer:

    Lord, we repent and submit the promise back to You. Teach us how to yield the promise to you daily (if necessary). Lord, please teach us how to continually search our hearts and check our motives for the pursuit of the promise in Jesus' name, amen. Feel free to add to this prayer point:

_____

_____

_____

_____

Notes & Overall Discoveries:

CHAPTER 11: HAGAR LEAVES

Genesis 16: 5-11 (AMPC): Then Sarai said to Abram, May [the responsibility for] my wrong and deprivation of rights be upon you! I gave my maid into your bosom, and when she saw that she was with child, I was contemptible and despised in her eyes. May the Lord be the judge between you and me.6 But Abram said to Sarai, See here, your maid is in your hands and power; do as you please with her. And when Sarai dealt severely with her, humbling and afflicting her, she [Hagar] fled from her.

Hagar's Question: Does Your God see me or does God really knows what's going on with me? Have you asked these questions of God? How has He confirmed His love and faithfulness towards you?

_____
_____
_____
_____

God's Answer – **Genesis 16: 7-11 (NIV):** But the Angel of the Lord found her by a spring of water in the wilderness on the road to Shur.8 And He said, Hagar, Sarai's maid, where did you come from, and where are you intending to go? And she said, I am running away from my mistress Sarai.9 The Angel of the Lord said to her, Go back to your mistress and [humbly] submit to her control.10 Also the Angel of the Lord said to her, I will multiply your descendants exceedingly, so that they shall not be numbered for multitude.11 And the Angel of the Lord continued, See now, you are with child and shall bear a son, and shall call his name Ishmael [God hears], because the Lord has heard and paid attention to your affliction.

How often have we asked God, if He sees and or knows what going on with us? God has an intimate knowledge of what's going on, He even knows the hidden intent and motives of man.

Genesis 16:13 (AMPC): So she called the name of the Lord Who spoke to her, You are a God of seeing, for she said, Have I [not] even here [in the wilderness] looked upon Him Who sees me [and lived]? Or have I here also seen [the future purposes or designs of] Him Who sees me?

Our time with Him (intimate or quiet time) can highlight His concern for us and undercover the truth of the scriptures and in particular this scripture:

Psalm 138:8 (KJ21): 8 The Lord will perfect that which concerneth me; Thy mercy, O Lord, endureth forever; forsake not the works of Thine own hands.

I like the old translation better, because God revealed something awesome to me. He said to me that EVERYTHING that is a concern to you, is a concern to Me (from your hair follicles to your toenails). Everything that could be a worry or a concern to you, is a concern to Me and that is why He asked that we cast our cares and worries upon Him. I like the following translations of this scripture:

1 Peter 5:7 (TLB): 7 Let him have all your worries and cares, for he is always thinking about you and watching everything that concerns you.

1 Peter 5:7 (AMP): 7 casting all your cares [all your anxieties, all your worries, and all your concerns, once and for all] on Him, for He cares about you [with deepest affection, and watches over you very carefully].

In those moments when we are going through trials and tribulations, the question is not really if God cares, but a request for demonstration: God show Yourself strong to Your people. Lord, let us look with expectancy for Your presence and the working of Your spirit in our lives.

Questions:

What is the trial and or tribulation revealing about you or God?

_____
_____
_____
_____

Additionally, what is the trial revealing about our character and posture of obedience?

_____
_____
_____
_____

Prayer:

> Lord, thank You that You prove to be BIG enough for the questions, help us not to shy away from asking You. In those times of inquiry, You are faithful to SHOW UP and SHOW US how You are in the details **Psalm 138:8 (AMPC)**. We should not anticipate that You will answer in the means and ways in which we desire but we can be assured of Your presence and Your promise to walk through these times with us. Let us confidently approach You, knowing that You are already working it out for our good. Thank You, that You do not leave us without (comforting, instructing, guiding, and perfecting us) in Jesus' name. Feel free to add to this prayer point:

_____
_____
_____
_____

Notes & Overall Discoveries:

CHAPTER 12: SECONDARY PROMISES & COUNTERFEITS

When we subvert God's way, we get an inferior portion of the promise or a counterfeit. **Genesis 16: 14-16 NIV:** Therefore, the well was called Beer-lahai-roi [A well to the Living One Who sees me]; it is between Kadesh and Bered.15 And Hagar bore Abram a son, and Abram called the name of his son whom Hagar bore Ishmael.16 Abram was eighty-six years old when Hagar bore Ishmael.

    God is so faithful to keep His word in all things. When He told Abram your descendants will be as the sand and stars; He meant the seed of your loins will seed nations. Although, Hagar is the substitute and an inferior method of the promise, God still cares for her, and God still honors His promise concerning Abram seed. Ishmael is a portion of the secondary promise that God gave to Abraham. Counterfeits are produced when we circumvent God's will and way in which to fulfill the promise. Some of our actions produce Hagar(s) and Ishmael(s) in our lives, and if we are not careful, we will be bound to take care of and nurture them. Those Hagar(s) and Ishmael(s) were never the intended promise; thus, they should not take up the focus, energy, and or resources that God has allotted for the authentic promise. Authentic promises have Kingdom intent.

    Hagar(s) and Ishmael(s) are birthed out of human solutions which do not necessarily produce Kingdom byproducts such as salvation, healing, and deliverance. God's intervention, due to His care and faithfulness to the promise, produces salvation from death and destruction. However, we should be mindful to care as much for Hagar and Ishmael as God did. Our actions may warrant that we must reject and or abandon Hagar and Ishmael (secondary promise) in pursuit of Sarai and Isaac. We should be very careful not to produce substitutes or counterfeits because they do not mirror actions of a submitted life, nor will they produce fulfillment of the same magnitude as Kingdom-purposed-promises.

Questions:

> Have any of your decisions or choices resulted in secondary promises, substitutes, or counterfeits? If so, are you still caring for those secondary promises or counterfeits?
>
> _____
> _____
> _____
> _____
>
> If not, how did you handle the secondary promise or counterfeit with care as directed by God?
>
> _____
> _____
> _____
> _____

Prayer:

> Lord, thank You for your faithfulness. We receive your authentic promise and reject all counterfeits. Change our appetites so that we desire the things that you want for us and removed the fear that "when we submit it all the thing that You want most for us, will not be the thing that we want for ourselves." Build and heal our trust in You, in Jesus' name, Amen. Feel free to add to this prayer point:
>
> _____
> _____
> _____
> _____

<u>Notes & Overall Discoveries:</u>

CHAPTER 13: NAME AND NATURE CHANGE

Genesis 17:1-5 (AMPC): When Abram was ninety-nine years old, the Lord appeared to him and said, I am the Almighty God; walk and live habitually before Me and be perfect (blameless, wholehearted, complete). 2 And I will make My covenant (solemn pledge) between Me and you and will multiply you exceedingly. 3 Then Abram fell on his face, and God said to him, 4 As for Me, behold, My covenant (solemn pledge) is with you, and you shall be the father of many nations. 5 Nor shall your name any longer be Abram [high, exalted father]; but your name shall be Abraham [father of a multitude], for I have made you the father of many nations.

I noted that God changed Abram's name. It is customary when God changes the character of a man and or woman, He changes the name. Thus, He changes what the man and or woman should answer to. For example, if a person was in bondage to lying under a name like Jacob, then the name change to Israel would signify freedom from lying to an identity of truth telling. As Israel, "my name is truth," I can no longer answer to the lie in the name or the carnal identity of Jacob any longer. There is a lot of significance in a name. Abram was already to be an exalted father; however, Abraham bespoke of the promise to be the Father of nations. Spiritually, I wonder what my name has been changed from and to.

Recently, I wrote a blog entitled

What name am I answering to?

The work that I do comes from who I am. Who am I?

I, like others have been searching and or claiming myself. Most of my life I have been told who I am by what I do. Or, more importantly, what others thought I should do. I have learned to be a human doing; not necessarily a human being. What do others want me to do? Well, because I am a woman, there are things that I should do as a woman; however, I was told there are things that I should not do as a woman. I can tell you one of the countless incidents with my male friends.

One of my dear friends wanted to do an act of kindness by having my oil changed for me. I told him that I would take care of the oil change. My gracious friend responded with, "Why are you trying to be a man." I was stung with the realization that we had missed each other. I, a person that lived as a single cell, independent, and self-sufficient, did not think that there was someone that I could depend on. While he may have been stung by the sting of rejection of a well-meaning gesture, the name independence which I had been answering to for most of my life, required me to "do" actions that displayed independence.

I have answered to the names that I have been called. Some of the names I respect, for instance Njeri Monik Pringle. Njeri is of Swahili origin, and it means warrior, warrior's daughter, loyal, faithful, hardworking, and devoted. I am all of those, and I am a person that advocates and fights for others and what I value. I am a daughter of two people who also fight (dad) and fought(mother) for righteous causes. I am loyal, faithful, hardworking, and devoted. Monik (or Monique) was initially slated to be Mona, but my courageous dad (who wanted to give his kids names with meanings) intervened and thus Monik is a happy compromise.

In researching, Monique is a variation of Monica. In looking at the break down of Monica "monos": "hermit, single, or to advise or warn. (http://www.babynamespedia.com, 2015)." I have lived my life singularly; probably religiously with the warning to self that singleness keeps me safe, which is still answering to my name of independence. Pringle also has a meaning: to cause "tingling in", I can provoke thought so I hope that the tingling is happening in the brain and or the heart.

What's in a name? Other names that I answer to have not been spoken out loud. These are the names that I have called myself. Recently, I have been challenging my students and myself: "If you would not say it out loud to someone else, stop saying it to yourself." Sometimes, I have added a disclaimer on that statement because some of my students may say it out loud to someone else. But this is a challenge, as I have looked in the mirror sometimes and said you are ugly, or if you fix or hide this you will be more beautiful.

However, who am I trying to look beautiful for when the person that is most important has already passed judgment? I showed my students the Dove Real Beauty Sketch: You are More Beautiful Than You Think (2013). The power of what we perceive and what the rest of the world sees is tremendous and has such an impact on our expectations of what we deserve. What we are called early on will shape the image we project on ourselves.

Those names will shape what names we are prone to answer to. I remember being made fun of and hearing all those names that I tried to silence through my "doing" and not "being." My being had been rejected earlier on by others; so, for the most part my "being" had been rejected by me. Doing became the avenue of acceptance; within my own capabilities I can "do" a lot of things. But in the end, I can only be "ME." Me is more than good enough even while doing nothing.

Questions:

What are some names that people call you that you should not answer to?

_____

_____

_____

_____

What are some names you should stop calling yourself?

_____

_____

_____

_____

What or who does God call you? (fearfully and wonderfully made, blessed and highly favored, the head and not the tail, more than a conqueror, my child)? I love that David agree with God (and my soul, so knows it), specifically "what God had proclaimed over him."

_____

_____

_____

_____

Can we imagine what God feels when He has given us a new name and character and sometimes, we answer to our old name and nature?

_____

_____

How can we stand fast in our new name and nature? What can we do to remind ourselves that in Christ Jesus we have been made a new creature fit for glorious things?

Prayer:

Lord, please mark us in a way that we see ourselves as You see us. Help remind us of our identities, let us not behold our faces and forget what we have seen **James 1:24 (NIV)**. Keep uprooting the lies that our previous names and natures spoke over our intended futures and hopes. We will continue to seek Your face so that we can become and behold who You are making us to be in Jesus' name, amen. Feel free to add to this prayer point:

Notes & Overall Discoveries:

CHAPTER 14: THE BLESSING, PROMISE, COVENANT WITH GOD

Genesis 17: 6-9 (NIV) And I will make you exceedingly fruitful and I will make nations of you, and kings will come from you. 7 And I will establish My covenant between Me and you and your descendants after you throughout their generations for an everlasting, solemn pledge, to be a God to you and to your posterity after you. 8 And I will give to you and to your posterity after you the land in which you are a stranger [going from place to place], all the land of Canaan, for an everlasting possession; and I will be their God. 9 And God said to Abraham, As for you, you shall therefore keep My covenant, you and your descendants after you throughout their generations.

The proclamation of generational blessings and even the Promised Land can have one asking when and how can this happen. Our God is interested in our posture or exaltation to Him as He makes or allows blessings to happen on our behalf. It is not Abraham who is approaching God to inquire of and or solicit; it is God presenting His heart through a promise to Abraham. Through this promise God is showcasing His majesty, love, care, and esteem of Abraham. His covenant was not a singular event and or blessing to be experienced by one; His blessing is a perpetual blessing upon generation upon generation (Kingdom intent).

As a single woman, without children, I can only imagine the impact of a generational blessing. Few can keep his or her promise to one individual throughout a lifetime, but to keep an infinite promise to strangers is unfathomable. The feat of keeping generational knowledge can be dauting…. great, great, great, great, great grandfather or kids have spanned or will span many generational before and after us. Thus, a multi-generational blessing and or curse can change the course of those yet born.

Questions:

    What have you gained from your heritage?

    _____

    _____

What have you passed on as a legacy? (Note: everyone can answer this question even non-parents, as everyone can leave a legacy)

___

What attributes of your lineage are you conscious of stopping in your generation? What attributes are your mindful to preserve and continue?

___

Brainstorm: Please take a moment to brainstorm other attributes that you want to be conscious of displaying and teaching.

___

Prayer:

Lord, please help us to differentiate between a Godly legacy (attributes, attitudes, etc.) and an ungodly legacy (attributes, attitudes, behaviors, etc.), help us to exchange. Lord, help us to be legacy minded and give us grace to contend for our Godly inheritance. In Jesus' name, amen. Feel free to add to this prayer point:

___

Chapter 15: Distinguishing those Set Aside for the Promise

Genesis 17:10-14 (AMPC): This is My covenant, which you shall keep, between Me and you and your posterity after you: Every male among you shall be circumcised. 11 And you shall circumcise the flesh of your foreskin, and it shall be a token or sign of the covenant (the promise or pledge) between Me and you. 12 He who is eight days old among you shall be circumcised, every male throughout your generations, whether born in [your] house or bought with [your] money from any foreigner not of your offspring. 13 He that is born in your house and he that is bought with your money must be circumcised; and My covenant shall be in your flesh for an everlasting covenant.14 And the male who is not circumcised, that soul shall be cut off from his people; he has broken My covenant.

God does something amazing in that the birthmarks He gives His children make us a peculiar people. We do things just a little bit different than the "norm." If we are called to be transformed to mirror our Father then there are "must do" things that showcase His character. Loving God and loving others are strong indications that we have chosen to keep those things which He said would identify us with, His promises and or covenants **John 13:35 (NIV)**. It is like having identical twins and putting a mark to make a distinction but then later observing their mannerism to see who is who.
Questions:

How do our mannerism help our Father to know that we are His?
_____
_____
_____
_____

How do we do those things which prompt the blessings of God:
_____
_____
_____
_____

Are we looking to make a withdrawal (to get God's promise, what He has for us without meeting the requirements)? For example, do we use the wrong pin number under a false name and or identity? This happens when we will not allow Him to change our character or nature. There are blessings even Jacob could not have until he became Israel? What are the requirements for your promise(s)? What is God doing in you to change your name and nature?

_____

_____

_____

_____

Circumcision is the practice of cutting something away. Physical and spiritual circumcision have implications which can be both pleasing and displeasing to God. Additionally, both circumcisions may affect our physical and or spiritual health. In several instances, He reminded the people of God about their covenantal responsibility of circumcision (Abraham, David, and Moses, etc.). Now in examining the physical benefits and or costs of circumcision versus non-circumcision, I have utilized the following excerpt from Healthychildren.org (2015):

> Circumcision has been practiced as a religious rite for thousands of years. In the United States, most boys are circumcised for religious or social reasons. At present, there is discussion over whether circumcision is advisable from a medical standpoint. There are potential medical benefits to circumcision as well as risks. A recent analysis by the American Academy of Pediatrics concluded that the medical benefits of circumcision outweigh the risks. Studies have concluded that circumcised infants have a slightly lower risk of urinary tract infections, although these are not common in boys and occur less often in circumcised boys mostly in the first year of life. Neonatal circumcision also provides some protection from penile cancer, a very rare condition. Some research also suggests a reduced likelihood of developing sexually transmitted diseases and HIV infections in circumcised men, and possibly a reduced risk for cervical cancer in female partners of circumcised men. However, while there are potential medical benefits, the data are not sufficient to recommend

routine neonatal circumcision of all boys. We recommend that the decision to circumcise is one best made by parents in consultation with their pediatrician, taking into account what is in the best interests of the child, including medical, religious, cultural, and ethnic traditions and personal beliefs. (American Academy of Pediatrics via healthychildren.org, 2009; 2015).

He then spoke to the people about the circumcision of the heart, removing of those things which will bring infection and or disease to our relationship with God, others, and ourselves. God originally made circumcision as a way to distinguish His chosen people, and He even utilized circumcision to symbolize His adoption of the Gentiles into His family. Adoption allows us to be heirs with Christ and inheritors of the "promises of God."

Romans 2:25-29 (AMPC): Circumcision does indeed profit if you keep the Law; but if you habitually transgress the Law, your circumcision is made uncircumcision. 26 So if a man who is uncircumcised keeps the requirements of the Law, will not his uncircumcision be credited to him as [equivalent to] circumcision? 27 Then those who are physically uncircumcised but keep the Law will condemn you who, although you have the code in writing and have circumcision, break the Law. 28 For he is not a [real] Jew who is only one outwardly and publicly, nor is [true] circumcision something external and physical. 29 But he is a Jew who is one inwardly, and [true] circumcision is of the heart, a spiritual and not a literal [matter]. His praise is not from men but from God.

In examining the reasons to forgo circumcision, I would have to say that most of us are pain-avoidant. This is a reason why countless times we ignore medical or other conditions in hopes that they will go away. We, think that, like children if we do not acknowledge it, then it cannot be real. More importantly, we have assessed the pain involved in recovery and have chosen today's pain of unhealthiness. However, there is health and wholeness on the other side of this present pain, there is growth and access to things that we cannot access in this unhealthy state (Romans 8:18 NIV)
Questions:

What is God trying to cut away from you?

Have these things caused an infection of the heart, mind, or soul?

How can you trust God to yield His scalpel with precision?

Prayer:

    Lord, please amplify our faith and trust, that we may trust You to be precise when extracting things that cause infection in our relationship with You. Lord, we know that there is benefit on the other side of the pain. Help us not to resist as we desire to be good for and to You-Father, others, and ourselves in Jesus' name, amen. Feel free to add to this prayer point:

Notes & Overall Discoveries:

CHAPTER 16: CIRCUMCISED HEART VS. UNCIRCUMCISED HEART

Circumcised Heart - Deuteronomy 30:6 (NIV): The LORD your God will circumcise your hearts and the hearts of your descendants, so that you may love him with all your heart and with all your soul, and live.

Uncircumcised Heart - John 10:10 Amplified Bible (AMP): The thief comes only in order to steal and kill and destroy. I came that they may have and enjoy life, and have it in abundance [to the full, till it overflows].

God is asking that we cut away and or rid ourselves of the sin nature which separates us from communing and hearing from God. He wants us to separate ourselves from things, attitudes, people, situations, which decrease and or take away life and life more abundantly (liberty). Adam communed and heard from God daily; however, because the enemy sought to destroy God's design of an unashamed, untainted, relationship between God and us, sin was introduced.

The damage to communion stole our innocence and limitless ability to pursue our God. Now our pursuit is complicated by us engaging and fighting our enemy. When Adam and Eve were in the garden, the enemy only had access through observation; however, sin and or sinning gives him grounds and authority to hold us bound. Through sin, true death to our spiritual walk and possibly physical being becomes the byproduct of a posture of disobedience and rebellion.

Prayer

> Lord, we repent of our attachments to dead things, that rob us of life. Lord, we desire a circumcised heart, one in which You can dwell and work through us. We pray for your freedom. Any access that we have given the enemy, we ask that You help us recover and take back. These are areas where we were stripped -naked and vulnerable to the enemy. We also ask that You give us more territory, give us victory, let us reign with power and war on the behalf of others that need to be free (**Isaiah 61:1 NIV**). We bless You and thank You for our way of forgiveness, Your precious Son Jesus Christ. We thank You for His blood that has covered our sin and washed us so that we can be white as snow (pure before You) (**Isaiah 1:18 NIV**). We pray that You remove the

guilt and shame, as we desire to walk in the full freedom that You give us (much like Adam and Eve before the fall). We pray all of these things in Jesus' name, amen. Feel free to add to this prayer point:

_____
_____
_____
_____

Notes & Overall Discoveries:

CHAPTER 17: A NAME CHANGE FOR SARAI

Genesis 17: 15-16 (AMPC): And God said to Abraham, As for Sarai your wife, you shall not call her name Sarai; but Sarah [Princess] her name shall be.16 And I will bless her and give you a son also by her. Yes, I will bless her, and she shall be a mother of nations; kings of peoples shall come from her.

God told Abraham to no longer call his wife Sarai but to call her Sarah; just as God through name change prophetically called him to an identity of "Father of all Nations" so He called to the identity of Sarah to be "the Mother of Nations."

Questions:

Has God prophetically called you by a new name? Have you answered to this new name?

_____
_____
_____
_____

Did God allow someone else to acknowledge this new name and or nature before you? Abram knew Sarai's new name before she did.

_____
_____
_____
_____

Does that have a bearing on how well you accept your new name and nature? Does it matter if you hear it from God directly, or if God entrusts others with that information before you?

_____
_____
_____
_____

Has he embedded His promise and purpose in this new name and or identity?

_____
_____
_____
_____

If you can do it in your own strength, knowledge, and or ability this probably is not the totality of the promise and or purpose. If you have to rely on God and His direction, provision, and vision (which ignites faith) then this sings of purpose. If it is bigger than your eye and what you can see, then it's just right for His vision and provision.

Questions:

Could Sarah get a full vision of being the origin of Kings?

_____
_____
_____
_____

Can you see yourself as the lender (possible president of the bank) and not a borrower?

_____
_____
_____
_____

What keeps us from getting a greater vision of ourselves in the light of the promises that God has for us (examples: low self-esteem, distorted self-image, distorted view of the Promise Giver and Maker, God)?

_____
_____
_____
_____

Do we think ourselves unworthy? If so, what qualifies us? If not, what disqualifies us from God's blessings and promises?

Why do some of us like to try to pay for the promise through works to feel as if we have "earned it" and that it is just not a "gift" from God?

Could you ever earn the titles that God calls you, for instance Sarai (my princesses) to Sarah (princess)? How does the graciousness of God impact your ability to receive His gifts and promises?

When we have a distorted sense of self and have not accepted our place or the identity that God is calling us to, then we see a reflection of ourselves only. The reflection of self only mirrors our current state and not the projected image of what God is making us into. We must seek God to see what He sees when He sees us. Question:

What are some ways that you replace the lies of the enemy with the word of God (example: David: **Psalm 119: 11 (NIV):** I have hidden your word in my heart that I might not sin not against thee)

Prayer:

> Lord give us Your eyes and heart. Lord, let us experience the love that You have for us in such tangible ways as to negate every distortion of who You are calling us to be. We surrender our mirrors or pictures of ourselves in exchange for the wonderous beings that You are making us into. We love You, teach us to love ourselves so that we can truly love others as You intended. Thank You for the love in which to love You, others, and ourselves. Heal and uproot any lies of the enemy that perpetuate distorted truth, Lord, help us replace it with Your words in Jesus' name, amen.
>
> **2 Corinthians 10:5 KJV**: casting down imaginations and every high thing that exalteth itself against the knowledge of God, and bringing into captivity every thought to the obedience of Christ.
>
> Feel free to add to this prayer point:
>
> _____
> _____
> _____
> _____

Notes & Overall Discoveries:

CHAPTER 18: BECOMING

Once I wrote a poem that depicts the struggle between our present self and the one that we are becoming:

The Me that I Am Becoming

In this space of in between

I am envisioning the me that I will be

and the me that I was

in relation to the me that I am now

The reflections are not the same

I see some outlines of what I was and a projected image of what I am becoming

The question today, is who am I?

Who am I today?

Not just to myself, but who am I to those who share this life with me

Am I a vapor?

Am I a rock?

Am I a shoulder?

Am I a blade?

Who am I?

Who am I to the one that is making me into the one that I am becoming?

Am I His child?

Am I His Israel in the wilderness?

Am I His bride or a harlot (like Hosea's wife)?

Am I an Oasis or am I a barren land?

I have been and probably will be all of those things to all of those people that I love

and who love me

But in loving me, I long for the freedom to just be

to be the vapor, rock, shoulder, blade, child, bride, and harlot

To be the reflection of my past me, the materialization of my current me, and the projected image of who I am becoming (Prayer: let me be the me that You are making Lord).

For many of us, the in-between is the place we like least. We have seen the growth from who we once were, and we can see glimpses of who we are becoming. The in-between is the place of preparation that we would like to forgo. In previous chapters we discussed circumcision, the in-between versions of ourselves which require a pruning in order to bear fruit **John 15:1-8 (AMPC)**.

Prayer:

> Lord, please keep giving us both the vision of who we were and who You are making us to be. Also, please grant us grace to stand and submit to the pruning necessary to "become." Lord, becoming who You have called us to be is our desire. Let us reach maturity in You by abiding in a posture of obedience and submission in Jesus' name, amen. Feel free to add to this prayer point:
>
> _____
> _____
> _____
> _____

<u>Notes & Overall Discoveries:</u>

CHAPTER 19: TOO GOOD TO BE TRUE

Genesis 17: 17-19 (AMPC) Then Abraham fell on his face and laughed, and said in his heart, "Shall a child be born to a man who is a hundred years old? And shall Sarah, who is ninety years old, bear a child?" 18 And Abraham said to God, "Oh, that Ishmael [my firstborn] might live before You!" 19 But God said, "No, Sarah your wife shall bear you a son indeed, and you shall name him Isaac (laughter); and I will establish My covenant with him for an everlasting covenant and with his descendants after him.

Abraham's posture is not one of acceptance and submission; it is more like a rejection of the promise based upon his current view of himself. Lord, this promise cannot be for me, do You not see what my current circumstance looks like: do You see my bank account, my physical composure (health, appearance, etc.), my educational background, and my age? The list reads just like the employment anti-discrimination list (Department of Justice, 2015):

> "Federal laws prohibit discrimination based on a person's national origin, race, color, religion, disability, sex, and familial status. Laws prohibiting national origin discrimination make it illegal to discriminate because of a person's birthplace, ancestry, culture or language. This means people cannot be denied equal opportunity because they or their family are from another country, because they have a name or accent associated with a national origin group, because they participate in certain customs associated with a national origin group, or because they are married to or associate with people of a certain national origin" (Department of Justice, 2015).

How many times have we discriminated against ourselves and relinquished the rights that have been afforded us? We have looked at our race, perceived or real disabilities, birthplace, or culture? We say in our hearts like Abraham: I cannot have a family because of the family background in which I was raised. I cannot be wealthy because everyone in my family is poor, etc. Others may even put stipulations of what we can do based upon the "places we come from." Much like Moses, God will send an answer for every deficiency we perceive ourselves to have, He can also make the deficiency work for Kingdom purpose.

Questions:

Have you ever tried to disqualify yourself from a task or endeavor that God has called you to do?

_____
_____
_____
_____

How did or are you overcoming your self-doubt?

_____
_____
_____
_____

How can you still have self-doubt, but trust in the God that is sending you?

_____
_____
_____
_____

Prayer:

Lord, we pray that we remind ourselves of your Dunamis power that works in us **(Ephesians 3:20 NIV)**. You are greater, Lord, we magnify you above any perceived deficiencies in Jesus' mighty name, amen. Feel free to add to this prayer point:

_____
_____
_____
_____

Notes & Overall Discoveries:

CHAPTER 20: OLD FRIENDS VS. NEW NAME & NATURE

John 1:45-46 (AMP): 45 Philip found Nathanael and told him, "We have found the One Moses in the Law and also the Prophets wrote about—Jesus from Nazareth, the son of Joseph [according to public record]."46 Nathanael answered him, "Can anything good come out of Nazareth?" Philip replied, "Come and see."

Nathanael response is like so many people in our lives that were there at the beginning and saw us only as Abram and not Abraham, Sarai and not Sarah. They have not received the vision and or projections of Abraham and Sarah, Father and Mother of nations.

Questions:

Do you have family and or friends who resist your process of change, if so, how are you balancing your love for them and desire to change?

_____
_____
_____
_____

Do they want you to be who you were (someone other than yourself) and not who God is calling you to be? How is that impacting your growth?

_____
_____
_____
_____

What name(s) do they keep calling you, in light of the fact that God has already changed your nature and name?

_____
_____
_____
_____

What things do they still want you to identify with or want your identity to be built upon? Example: activities that you no longer engage in, or focuses that are no longer the priority?

_____
_____
_____
_____

Create a list of the things that God is calling you to do now, you can make a parallel list (things you did vs. things you do).

Things I Did	*Things I Do*

Are you guilty of calling someone else their old name or by their old nature? How can you practice seeing them rightly and calling them by their God-given identity (example: My pastor calls men and women (men or women of God)?

_____
_____
_____
_____

<u>Notes & Overall Discoveries:</u>

CHAPTER 21: SECONDARY OR INFERIOR PROMISE

Genesis 17:20-22 (AMPC): 20 As for Ishmael, I have heard and listened to you; behold, I will bless him, and will make him fruitful and will greatly multiply him [through his descendants]. He will be the father of twelve princes (chieftains, sheiks), and I will make him a great nation. 21 But My covenant [My promise, My solemn pledge], I will establish with Isaac, whom Sarah will bear to you at this time next year." 22 And God finished speaking with him and went up from Abraham.

God blessed Ishmael because he was of Abraham's seed and a partial fulfillment of making the promise (your descendants as dust or the stars). However, there is a limit; God does not say, as He does of Isaac, that this is a perpetual blessing and promise. The blessing is for 12 princes (chieftains and or sheiks). God did this to honor Abraham's seed.

Questions:

> How have we asked God to bless and perpetuate an inferior or secondary promise (jobs, relationships, lifestyles)?
>
> _____
> _____
> _____
> _____

Prayer & Task:

> Have you asked God to bless a secondary promise and then got upset with Him because it is a limited or inferior promise? If so, let's repent together. Lord, we repent of asking You to bless an inferior promise when we know that You have the best for us. Change our desires and appetites to desire what You have for us in Jesus' name. Here is an example: If God wants to bless you with a Mercedes but you want a Toyota Camry; God may bless you with the Camry but will wait for you to lift your eyes to the "superior promise." He is patience so He will wait until your desires mature. That is when He will grant you the desires of your heart because they are actually His desires for you. Please make

a list of superior promises that you would let God enact through and in your life.

_____
_____
_____
_____

Notes & Overall Discoveries:

CHAPTER 22: OBEDIENCE & HONOR TO COVENANT

Genesis 17: 23-27 (AMP): Then Abraham took Ishmael his son, and all the servants who were born in his house and all who were purchased with his money, every male among the men of Abraham's household, and circumcised the flesh of their foreskin the very same day, as God had said to him. 24 So Abraham was ninety-nine years old when he was circumcised. 25 And Ishmael his son was thirteen years old when he was circumcised. 26 On the very same day Abraham was circumcised, as well as Ishmael his son. 27 All the men [servants] of his household, both those born in the house and those purchased with money from a foreigner, were circumcised along with him [as the sign of God's covenant with Abraham].

At times we want to get God's stuff without doing it God's way, and He cannot bless rebellion. There is no protection within rebellion and disobedience. Recently, my sister has been saying that God will hide me but will not hide stuff from me (Wilkerson, 2015). The posture of obedience positions us to hear from God while hiding and abiding behind His wings and in His presence **Psalms 91:1 (KJV)**.

Questions:

How can we stay hidden while still in pursuit of the Seed of Promise?

_____
_____
_____
_____

How can we let God go before us and make our legs like hind feet so that we may step where He has already step **Psalm 37:23 (NKJV):** The steps of a good man are ordered by the LORD: and he delighteth in his way; **Habakkuk 3:19 (NKJV):** The Sovereign LORD is my strength; He makes my feet like the feet of a deer, He enables me to tread on the heights. **Psalms 18:33 (KJV):** He maketh my feet like hinds' feet, and setteth me upon my high places.

_____
_____
_____
_____

Prayer:

> Lord, please order our steps and hide us under Your wings until it is time. We yield and trust You in this process of promise maturity. Identify anything in us that hinders promise fulfillment and give us the grace to address hinderances in Jesus' name, amen. Feel free to add to this prayer point:

_____
_____
_____
_____

Notes & Overall Discoveries:

CHAPTER 23: HOSPITALITY
An Offering of Grace

Genesis 18:1-4 (AMPC): Now the Lord appeared to Abraham by the terebinth trees of Mamre [in Hebron], while he was sitting at the tent door in the heat of the day. 2 When he raised his eyes and looked up, behold, three men were standing [a little distance] from him. When he saw them, he ran from the tent door to meet them and bowed down [with his face] to the ground, 3 and Abraham said, "My lord, if now I have found favor in your sight, please do not pass by your servant [without stopping to visit].

Question:

> Could the three men represent the total personage of God: Father, Son, and Holy Spirit?

_____

_____

_____

_____

Genesis 18: 4-8 (AMPC): 4 Please let a little water be brought [by one of my servants] and [you may] wash your feet, and recline and rest comfortably under the tree. 5 And I will bring a piece of bread to refresh and sustain you; after that you may go on, since you have come to your servant." And they replied, "Do as you have said." 6 So Abraham hurried into the tent to Sarah, and said, "Quickly, get ready three measures of fine meal, knead it and bake cakes." 7 Abraham also ran to the herd and brought a calf, tender and choice, and he gave it to the servant [to butcher], and he hurried to prepare it. 8 Then he took curds and milk and the calf which he had prepared, and set it before the men; and he stood beside them under the tree while they ate.

The above is an illustration of Abraham in fellowship and communion with God and or angelic Beings. Most commentaries agree that the three were heavenly beings, but some say that they were angels, while some say that the Son of God was among them. However, Keith Krell (2006) says that we miss much through translation because the original Hebrew text states that Abraham address the man as "My Lord" (as in my

God) not as "my lord and or sir" (2006). I am sure that we too have been unaware of heavenly visitation.

Prayer:
> Lord, I pray that You make us sensitive and discerning to our encounters with You, the Holy Spirit, and the Heavenly Hosts in Jesus' name, amen. Feel free to add to this prayer point:
>
> _____
> _____
> _____
> _____

Notes & Overall Discoveries:

CHAPTER 24: ANGELIC VISITATION

Hebrews 13:2 Amplified Bible (AMP) 2 Do not neglect to extend hospitality to strangers [especially among the family of believers—being friendly, cordial, and gracious, sharing the comforts of your home and doing your part generously], for by this some have entertained angels without knowing it.

But Abraham's hospitality is a gift of honor, an honor to the messengers of God, those that dispense God's grace and wrath. We see countless times where angels have come to the rescue of men (Abram, Jeremiah, Daniel, Elijah, Elisha, Mary & Joseph, Saul/Paul, Elisha (those with us more than those against us). We also see when angels dispense God's wrath (Sodom & Gormorrah, and Revelation (when the seals will be broken). Wesley Duewel (1986) speaks of angels in the service of God:

> "God's holy Angels are your invisible prayer expediters. Scripture teaches that the total number of God's Angels is beyond human numbering (Heb 12:22). Their primary responsibility as created beings is to worship and serve Christ (Heb, 1:4, 6-7). Secondarily, they are assigned by God to serve "those who will inherit salvation" (Heb, 1:14). Angels have a keen interest in all that concerns us, because we are important to Christ. We are His church, His bride" (Duewel, 1986).

When I was young, I remember my mom telling us a story of an angelic rescue. At age 5, my family (dad, mom, sister, brother and myself) moved to Ohio, in route our van broke down in the middle of the highway. My mom was in distressed, we were in a very vulnerable position. A stranger appeared out of nowhere, he also was concerned about the potential danger. He helped my dad move the van to safety, my mother turned to thank him, and he was gone. Had we encountered an angel unaware? Question:

> Are you conscious of angelic activity in your life or the lives of others? If so, how does it impact your faith in God's ability to rescue and deliver you?

_____
_____
_____
_____

Isaiah 46:4 (KJV): Even to your old age and gray hairs. I am he; I am he who will sustain you. I have made you and I will carry you; I will sustain you and I will rescue you.

God gave me the above scripture when I was in a place of extreme distress and anxiousness. The Lord provided an illustration in that He was saying from birth, through life (all of it), until death He is with me every step of the way. He gave me the scripture as a reminder that He is the same God (**Hebrews 13:8 NIV**: yesterday, today, and forevermore). The reminder was necessary in that He called me to remember that He has ALWAYS rescued and delivered me. Much like David, I needed to remember that the situation does not determine the character and faithfulness of my God (God is ALWAYS good)! The stance forces me to seek God's face (His presence) more than I seek His hands (His resources). Additionally, the stance calls to the spirit of gratitude wherein I am learning to count it all joy.

James 1:2-8 (NIV): 2 Consider it pure joy, my brothers and sisters, whenever you face trials of many kinds, 3 because you know that the testing of your faith produces perseverance. 4 Let perseverance finish its work so that you may be mature and complete, not lacking anything. 5 If any of you lacks wisdom, you should ask God, who gives generously to all without finding fault, and it will be given to you. 6 But when you ask, you must believe and not doubt, because the one who doubts is like a wave of the sea, blown and tossed by the wind. 7 That person should not expect to receive anything from the Lord. 8 Such a person is double-minded and unstable in all they do.

Prayer:

> Lord, help us to count it all joy and seek You in times of distress; knowing that You are faithful to deliver us. Lord, when we are asking, and our faith is not strong – heal our unbelief so that we may have singleness of heart and mind. In Jesus' name, amen. Feel free to add to this prayer point:
>
> _____
> _____
> _____
> _____

CHAPTER 25: PROCLAMATION OF THE PROMISE
Gifts Make Room

Proverbs 18:16 (KJV): 16 A man's gift maketh room for him, and bringeth him before great men.

Question:

    What gift is God using to make room for you?

_____
_____
_____
_____

Abraham's Gift of Honor and Hospitality Positioned Him for a Blessing.

Genesis 18:9-10 (AMP): Then they said to him, "Where is Sarah your wife?" And he said, "There, in the tent." 10 He said, "I will surely return to you at this [s]time next year; and behold, Sarah your wife will have a son."

Question:

    What promise is God reminding you of, so that you may have faith to contend again for the fulfillment of that promise?

_____
_____
_____
_____

Genesis 18:11-15 (AMP): And Sarah was listening at the tent door, which was behind him. 11 Now Abraham and Sarah were old, well advanced in years; she was past [the age of] childbearing. 12 So Sarah laughed to herself [when she heard the Lord's words], saying, "After I have become old, shall I have pleasure and delight, my lord (husband) being also old?" 13 And the Lord asked Abraham, "Why did Sarah laugh [to herself], saying, 'Shall I really give birth [to a child] when I am so old?' 14 Is anything too difficult or too wonderful for the Lord? At the appointed time, when the season [for her delivery] comes, I will return to you and Sarah will have a son." 15 Then Sarah denied it, saying, "I did not laugh"; because she was afraid. And He (the Lord) said, "No, but you did laugh."

Our posture and response to the proclamation of promises is very important, since Sarah took the posture of unbelief which will later play out in her inability to trust God to fulfill this promise in His way and in His time.

Question:

What has God promise you, wherein you responded in laughter: I am too old, too _____, too_____, too_____, too_____?

Prayer:

Are you willing to TRUST Him to bring it to pass in His time and way? If so, let's repent for the stance of unbelief and doubt. Lord, we just ask for Your forgiveness as the man once said, we believe but heal our unbelief (**Mark 9:24 NIV**). Heal us in the areas where You are challenging growth of faith (beyond what we can perceive, achieve in our own strength, knowledge, or ability). Lord, we trust Your faithfulness, You pursued Abraham and Sarah and called them to remember (your authentic promise). You were faithful to remember it, even if they and or we have long since forgotten and or given up on that promise. We ask that You breathe on us and the promises and make them become life to us again. Lord allow us to pursue You and the promises that You have for us, let us not pursue the promise more than You, let us pursue You first and then watch those things be added to us (**Matthew 6:33 NIV**). In Jesus' name, amen. Feel free to add to this prayer point:

_____
_____
_____
_____

Chapter 26: Our Laughter

Our laughing, unbelief and doubt are not hidden from God. It is amplified in our posture, in our cool reserve -our wait and see stance. Note that the laughing and unbelieving posture is not a posture of (we do not see it but because of who You are Lord, we will trust You). Lord, because of Your faithfulness, You are bigger than all limitations that seem to try to cloud our view of faith. Here's an awesome except from Matthew Henry's Concise Commentary (1706) on Sarah's unbelief:

> "Where is Sarah thy wife? was asked. Note the answer, In the tent. Just at hand, in her proper place, occupied in her household concerns. There is nothing gained by gadding. Those who are in their proper place are most likely to receive comfort from God and his promised while there in the way of their duty, **Luke 2:8 (NIV)**. We are slow of heart to believe and need line upon line of the same purport. The blessings others have from common providence, believers have from the Divine promise, which makes them very sweet and very sure. The spiritual seed of Abraham owe their life, joy, hope, and all, to the promise. Sarah thinks this too good to be true; she laughed, and therefore cannot as yet find in her heart to believe it. Sarah laughed. We might not have thought there was a difference between Sarah's laughter and Abraham's, **Genesis 17:17 (NIV)**; but He who searches the heart, saw that the one sprung from unbelief, and the other from faith. She denied that she had laughed. One sin commonly brings in another, and it is not likely we shall strictly keep to truth, when we question the Divine truth. But whom the Lord loves he will rebuke, convict, silence, and bring to repentance, if they sin before him. **Genesis 18:16-22 (NIV)**.

We must understand that our reality is not TRUTH. Reality is perceived through limited senses: seeing, tasting, smelling, feeling, hearing, and even remembering. However, those senses are not the totality of our sense. We also enact spiritual senses for the spiritual world. Our natural senses can sometimes become a handicap or hindrance to the Holy Spirit Who is at work within us. Sometimes, the natural senses limit us and God to the circumstances and make the circumstances greater than the power of God. We see God's creation, galaxies, stars, us, and then question is He able to provide a solution to our perceived or real, big, or small problems (**Genesis 18:14**) Is there anything too hard for the Lord?

Question:

> What have you taken from under God's preview for fear that it is too big for Him?

_____

_____

_____

_____

Prayer:

> Lord, we repent for making our situations or circumstances greater than You. We magnify You, Lord, and submit to the process. We ask that You illuminate our understanding and partner with us in bringing a heaven solution to an earthly problem in Jesus' name, amen. Feel free to add to this prayer point:

_____

_____

_____

_____

Notes & Overall Discoveries:

Chapter 27: Truth Over Lies

Our job is to do the following: **2 Corinthians 10:5 (KJV):** 5 Casting down imaginations, and every high thing that exalteth itself against the knowledge of God, and bringing into captivity every thought to the obedience of Christ; another translation **2 Corinthians 10:5 (AMPC):** 5 [Inasmuch as we] refute arguments and theories and reasonings and every proud and lofty thing that sets itself up against the [true] knowledge of God; and we lead every thought and purpose away captive into the obedience of Christ (the Messiah, the Anointed One).

Our job is to assess how and when our realities do not align with the truth of God and what God says about a situation. We will forgo our realities in the face of truth. Truth becomes supreme and all the evidence we need is found in God's faithfulness. As the mind is the start and end of any battles or endeavors, it is important to first win control over who and what leads our thinking. As an educator, I have often said that "we do nothing, mindlessly." For example "veggie out" is still feeding yourself. In learning to control our mind, we are often led to guard our heart by also guarding our eye and ear gates.

Questions:

>When reality does not look like God's truth concerning you, how do you align the two? Additionally, how do you guard your heart, eye, and ear gates?
>
>_____
>_____
>_____
>_____

Prayer:

>Lord, give us a heightened discernment so that we may both recognize the wiles of the enemy but also Your way of escape **(I Corinthians 10:13 NIV).** Help us to put on the whole armor that we may be ready to fight, guard, and protect ourselves and Your promises **(Ephesians 6:11-18 NIV).** Help us to fight from the place of victory that You have already paid for through Your sacrifice on the cross **(Acts 2:31 NIV)** in Jesus' name, amen.

Chapter 28: Can God Trust Us Enough to Tell Us or Show Us His Plans for Us?

Genesis 18: 17-18 (AMPC): And the Lord said, Shall I hide from Abraham [My friend and servant] what I am going to do, 18 Since Abraham shall surely become a great and mighty nation, and all the nations of the earth shall be blessed through him and shall bless themselves by him?

Remember Sarah's doubt in **Genesis 18 (NIV)**. Additionally, we must remember that this was a reminder for Sarah as she was told the promise at the time of her name change (mother of nations). Is it a good thing that God asks if He can trust us with what He has in His heart to do for us? If God revealed all, for some it leads to obedience while for others it may lead to trying to manifest what God has told us in the spirit through earthly means. Our posture may change to one in which we pursue the promise more than the Promise Giver.

Questions:

What are indicators that we are chasing the promise more than God?

_____
_____
_____
_____

How can we recalibrate ourselves so that we can keep God first?

_____
_____
_____
_____

In my life, I have been guilty of the pursuit of the fulfillment of the promise. My achiever personality pushes me to "get it done" so that I can "cross it off the list." Patience must have her perfect work.

Prayer:

> Lord, please help us not to move ahead of You and create counterfeits. Let us not lag, let us pursue You so that we will be in alignment with Your steps. Lord, we seek You first. We will not place any idol before You **Exodus 20:2 (NIV)** In Jesus' name, amen. Feel free to add to this prayer point:

_____
_____
_____
_____

<u>Notes & Overall Discoveries:</u>

Chapter 29: Intimacy & Obedience Foster Trust

Genesis 18: 19 (AMPC): For I have known (chosen, acknowledged) him [as My own], so that he may teach and command his children and the sons of his house after him to keep the way of the Lord and to do what is just and righteous, so that the Lord may bring Abraham what He has promised him.

During the writing of this chapter, my home group Bible study challenged us to examine if God can trust us with the "greater than these things" (Heal the sick, raise the dead, and cleanse the lepers) (**John 14: 12 NIV; Matthew 10:8 (NIV)**? Questions posed by our leader were: How can we practically enact this principle and practices in our daily lives? What is stopping us from seeing and doing the greater than these things? Some of our responses included statements of strong belief in God but little belief in ourselves (individually, like Moses).

Others were of the mindset that it is during those times of intimacy (being known by God and knowing God-more than knowing about Him) where God can deal with our character and doubt. In really examining it, I think we came to the conclusion that it takes both intimacy and obedience; it is not enough for me to hear and know the Father's heart and will, if I do not act upon it. It is not enough to just hear His instructions for us to love, care, pray, preach the good news, heal the sick and bind up the brokenhearted, and proclaim liberty to the captives and prisoners (**Isaiah 61:1 NIV**). I must, we must move into action.

If my refusal or disobedience will not foster change in the lives of others, my disobedience will also not promote change in my character or transformation of my mind, will, and emotions. The lack of transformation does not enable me to look, act, smell, taste more like my Heavenly Father **Psalm 34:8 (NIV)**. Bill Johnson, Senior Pastor of Bethel Church in Redding, California (2008) stated that sometimes we do not see the greater than these things (healing manifestation, raising the dead, cleansing the leper) because we "pray instead of obey" (Johnson, 2008). Pastor Johnson (2008) stated that this positions us to blame God if the miracle does not occur; however, he stated that God has given us dominion. It is us that is on trial not God to see His Kingdom enacted in this earth (2008).

Additionally, Pastor Johnson (2008) makes a powerful statement that when we are intimately known of God and know God then His Kingdom's purpose and power flows out of us, and we enact Kingdom on Earth (2008). Illness is not a component of the Kingdom. When illness meets the power of the Holy Spirit it flees. Everything that is out of alignment with the Kingdom intent and purpose will bow to the power of the Holy Spirit. Alignment takes place when He is activated in us (not like lakes but like rivers….free to flow and overflow) (Johnson, 2008). We concluded in our Bible study that obedience in the everyday small things will allow God to trust us with the "greater than these things."

Questions:

Are you experiencing the "greater than these things" in your life? If not, honestly answer about your levels of intimacy and obedience to God in your daily life? More importantly, ask God about fears or barriers which may be hindering you from experiencing the "greater than these things."

_____
_____
_____
_____

How does the Holy Spirit enable you to command your day? In what ways do you seek His sovereignty in your life?

_____
_____
_____
_____

Does He flow like a river, bank like a lake, or trickle like a fountain in your life and daily encounters with others?

_____
_____
_____
_____

Please note that we have periods of all of the above, please answer as a demonstration of your current level of intimacy and power?

_____

_____

_____

_____

I am writing this as we are experiencing the 2nd round of COVID, I can truly say that I have traversed all and felt completely depleted. God has been so faithful to refresh and make the dead things live again. There is no judgement, this is just an assessment so that if there are any misalignments, we are calibrated back to the heart of God. Let's pray that we are empowered by the Holy Spirit much like the church of Pentecost. Please take this time to write your prayer or petition to God for His power to deliver you and others within your sphere of influence:

_____

_____

_____

_____

Chapter 30: God Judges Sin but Shows Mercy: Intercession

Genesis 18:20-33: 20 (AMPC) And the Lord said, Because the shriek [of the sins] of Sodom and Gomorrah is great and their sin is exceedingly grievous, 21 I will go down now and see whether they have one altogether [as vilely and wickedly] as is the cry of it which has come to Me; and if not, I will know.22 Now the [two] men turned from there and went toward Sodom, but Abraham still stood before the Lord. 23 And Abraham came close and said, Will You destroy the righteous (those upright and in right standing with God) together with the wicked? 24 Suppose there are in the city fifty righteous; will You destroy the place and not spare it for [the sake of] the fifty righteous in it?25 Far be it from You to do such a thing—to slay the righteous with the wicked, so that the righteous fare as do the wicked! Far be it from You! Shall not the Judge of all the earth execute judgment and do righteously? 26 And the Lord said, If I find in the city of Sodom fifty righteous (upright and in right standing with God), I will spare the whole place for their sake. 27 Abraham answered, Behold now, I who am but dust and ashes have taken upon myself to speak to the Lord. 28 If five of the fifty righteous should be lacking—will You destroy the whole city for lack of five? He said, If I find forty-five, I will not destroy it. 29 And [Abraham] spoke to Him yet again, and said, Suppose [only] forty shall be found there. And He said, I will not do it for forty's sake. 30 Then [Abraham] said to Him, Oh, let not the Lord be angry, and I will speak [again]. Suppose [only] thirty shall be found there. And He answered, I will not do it if I find thirty there. 31 And [Abraham] said, Behold now, I have taken upon myself to speak [again] to the Lord. Suppose [only] twenty shall be found there. And [the Lord] replied, I will not destroy it for twenty's sake. 32 And he said, Oh, let not the Lord be angry, and I will speak again only this once. Suppose ten [righteous people] shall be found there. And [the Lord] said, I will not destroy it for ten's sake. 33 And the Lord went His way when He had finished speaking with Abraham, and Abraham returned to his place.

Remember our previous inquiry, the questions concerning identity have been answered. It was God and two angelic beings. The angels journeyed on to Sodom and Gomorrah while God communed with Abraham. Abraham begins to intercede on behalf of the fallen world around him. Note: he was not petitioning God for their destruction; on the contrary, he was petitioning God for mercy.

Questions:

> How many times have I gone to "tell" on the world to my God instead of telling the world about my God?
>
> _____
> _____
> _____
> _____
>
> There will be times that the world will cause you some pain and or anguish. How can you cry out for mercy and not destruction?
>
> _____
> _____
> _____
> _____

There is a conviction to go and tell the world the good news, especially after writing this in 2015 and reading it in 2022. Our world is crying out to be told the good news of the Gospel of Jesus Christ. The Guardians of Promise is one way in which I help people grow, as people are also seeds of promise (God's promise – His Bride). As we experience help and deliverance, we are being cultivated into the authentic promise. We have a responsibility as well; we must also help others. Over the years, I have read the GOP and said this book ministers to me and I have heard the voice of God say that you did not write this book for yourself. This book is also a SOP, and it must have KINGDOM return on its investment.

Knowing God and being known by Him produces a different stance on condemnation versus conviction. We developed the same heart as God that "none should perish." Recently, I read a powerful quote which convicted me of my heart and passionate pursuit of God's bride. Charles H. Spurgeon (1834-1892) wrote the following excerpt (Carter, 1998, pp. 68):

> "If sinners be damned, at least let them leap to Hell over our dead bodies. And if they perish, let them perish with our arms wrapped about their knees, imploring

them to stay. If Hell must be filled, let it be filled in the teeth of our exertions, and let not one go unwarned and not prayed for."

This is such powerful imagery of what the spiritual warfare for souls must look like; more importantly, it shows the stance and preparation for God's people must take to fight on behalf of the lost. It is also a reminder that this is not an occasional pursuit. Just as God yearns to pursue us, we must also yearn to seek those whom He seeks. We must yearn to have a heart that says mercy, mercy, and more mercy be poured out before destruction. We must learn to say over our dead bodies will they go the way of no return.

Questions:

Who has God impressed upon your heart to pray for? This could be someone you know or do not know?

_____

_____

_____

_____

Has God given you the burden of intercession? Please note that this can also include people, groups, industries, countries, or nations?

_____

_____

_____

_____

How can we become more intentional about the concerns of God's heart?

_____

_____

_____

_____

Recently, many immigrants have come to these borders. At one time we also were sojourners within our faith walk. Here's God's heart **Deuteronomy 10:19 (AMPC)** "Therefore love the stranger and sojourner, for you were strangers and sojourners in the land of Egypt." We may disagree on immigration laws, practices, and procedures, but let us agree on the Father's heart of the treatment of His children. Let's us seek His face, His will, and execute with all diligence His care to His people.

Prayer:

> Lord, break our hearts with the things that break Your heart. Grow our love and capacity to love like You. Give us Your eyes, ears, and vision for Your people (Bride). Let us pursue her, as You have pursued us. Let us cultivate a fervency for the lost, dying, and hurting. Lord, please drive out the spirits of complacency and apathy that we have gained from a self-centered world view (place of privilege). Lord, we hurt because they hurt; we mourn because they mourn **Romans 12:15-16 (NIV)** in Jesus' name, amen. Feel free to add to this prayer point:

_____
_____
_____
_____

Notes & Overall Discoveries:

Chapter 31: God's Protection and Favor

Genesis 19: 1-10 (AMPC): It was evening when the two angels came to Sodom. Lot was sitting at Sodom's [city] gate. Seeing them, Lot rose up to meet them and bowed to the ground.2 And he said, my lords, turn aside, I beg of you, into your servant's house and spend the night and bathe your feet. Then you can arise early and go on your way. But they said, no, we will spend the night in the square. 3 [Lot] entreated and urged them greatly until they yielded and [with him] entered his house. And he made them a dinner [with drinking] and had unleavened bread which he baked, and they ate. 4 But before they lay down, the men of the city of Sodom, both young and old, all the men from every quarter, surrounded the house. 5 And they called to Lot and said, where are the men who came to you tonight? Bring them out to us, that we may know (be intimate with) them. 6 And Lot went out of the door to the men and shut the door after him 7 And said, I beg of you, my brothers, do not behave so wickedly. 8 Look now, I have two daughters who are virgins; let me, I beg of you, bring them out to you, and you can do as you please with them. But only do nothing to these men, for they have come under the protection of my roof. 9 But they said, Stand back! And they said, this fellow came in to live here temporarily, and now he presumes to be our] judge! Now we will deal worse with you than with them. So, they rushed at and pressed violently against Lot and came close to breaking down the door. 10 But the men [the angels] reached out and pulled Lot into the house to them and shut the door after him.

Earlier when choices were made, Lot chose the good land by sight. Making choices by sight can often lead us to places that we were never intended to go. I had a dream some time ago in which I came to a crossroad. The left choice contained a city full of chaos and violence. The right choice was a rural sanctuary; it was quiet and had a dirt road. I chose the right road for a few reasons: right directional and spiritually is right (directional dreams as illustrated within *Dream Language* by James & Michal Ann Goll (2006). The right also seemed to have the peace of God resting on it, and there was an indication that the right side would hold no work for me. There would be no work to gain and maintain the peace of God. I chose right, but I chose wrong.

My vehicle (ministry, as defined within *Dream Language*) quickly vanished, and I began to walk on this road that once had such assurance (Goll, 2006, p. 239). At some point in my journey, I noted that the area in which I was journeying begun to turn dark. It was not just physical darkness but also an intense spiritual darkness. I said in my heart "I will just turn around and go in the other direction," but that place too had also become too dark. The dream had several revelations concerning ministry or the avoidance of ministry. Other epiphanies gave me guidance in making major life decisions concerning employment and placement.

Later the nudges were proved to be valid. The dream showcased an important principle. Once I came to the stop sign, I had not consulted God. Somewhere in my "knower" I knew that the left place of chaos had work for me to do. I chose the avoidance of work and now I know it was work that God had ordained for me. The avoidance of God's work was an act of disobedience. In that place of disobedience, I had silenced the voice of God and became spiritually blind. My job became quite simple: heed the voice of God. No decision was too big or too small for which I needed God's guidance and hand. We witness character after character in the Bible that initially sought God's will. However, later they decided to do it their way and, without fail, it ended in disaster. As they acknowledge God's sovereignty, He revealed to them that His way and will are perfect.

Questions:

What decisions do you need to submit to God?

_____

_____

_____

_____

What work has God given you that you are avoiding? Sometimes the work is not work at all but an entering into His rest – but this also requires work as sometimes we do not do this easily. It is not too late to do the work, the actual work of entering His rest. Let's repent and put our hands back on the plow.

_____

_____

_____

_____

Prayer:

> Lord, we repent for not taking up our cross and walking out the work or rest that You have placed in our hands and hearts. Lord, please give us Your grace and empower us to return to the work or expand the work. Release us from guilt and shame, let Your love encompass us and breathe life back into Your vision and instruction of how to do the work that You have set before us. In Jesus' name, amen. Feel free to add to this prayer point:

_____
_____
_____
_____

<u>Notes & Overall Discoveries:</u>

Chapter 32: Submission: Mind over Matter

Hebrews 11:1-6 **(AMPC):** Now faith is the assurance (the confirmation, the title deed) of the things [we] hope for, being the proof of things [we] do not see and the conviction of their reality [faith perceiving as real fact what is not revealed to the senses]. 2 For by [faith trust and holy fervor born of faith] the men of old had divine testimony borne to them and obtained a good report. 3 By faith we understand that the worlds [during the successive ages] were framed (fashioned, put in order, and equipped for their intended purpose) by the word of God, so that what we see was not made out of things which are visible. 4 [Prompted, actuated] by faith Abel brought God a better and more acceptable sacrifice than Cain, because of which it was testified of him that he was righteous [that he was upright and in right standing with God], and God bore witness by accepting and acknowledging his gifts. And though he died, yet [through the incident] he is still speaking. 5 Because of faith Enoch was caught up and transferred to heaven, so that he did not have a glimpse of death; and he was not found, because God had translated him. For even before he was taken to heaven, he received testimony [still on record] that he had pleased and been satisfactory to God. 6 But without faith it is impossible to please and be satisfactory to Him. For whoever would come near to God must [necessarily] believe that God exists and that He is the rewarder of those who earnestly and diligently seek Him [out].

Recently, God has asked me to do some radical things that have taken a larger measure of faith. Throughout the process I have been learning to trust Him more and more. In the new walk, I have had some financial difficulties. My automatic instinct was first, that people (family, friends, and God) knew my need and that they should be moved by it. But I felt a restraint when asking people for help, God wanted to prove Himself to me. I did not ask others for help; instead, I planted a seed in church and was blessed with five times that amount. This illustration is not about the "name it, claim it" or even about sowing and reaping as much as it is about the posture of obedience and allowing God to reign over every circumstance.

I am learning to make God bigger and put circumstance in a proper perspective. Financial gain or lack must not move me more than God. My foundation is built on the fact that He is (God exist) and that He is…..I AM (all that is desired and needed).

My foundation is built on what He is…present in the situation and circumstance with me; I am not alone. He has all the resources that I need when I turn and say, "Father help me." The financial blessing, I mentioned earlier occurred in the company of my Christian brothers and sisters. This moment could have led to a type of shame, as my need was on display. However, I gloried and glory in the fact that God is in the details, and everything that is a concern to me is a concern to Him **Psalm 138:8 (KJV)**. The enemy would allow us to suffer in silence with pride, but vulnerability and transparency bring health and healing to the receiver and the giver of grace. One act of faith becomes testimony for everyone who views the act of faith and obedience.

The testimonies themselves become prophecies for others to claim. It helps us believe God for greater. We start believing God for ourselves and others when we see the manifestation of God's activity and presence within our situation. We can tell others that they too can trust God to take care of them in the same or greater manner in which He has taken care of us. They can expect God to heal them in the same or greater manner in which He has healed us. Some of us have been healed from cancer, diabetes, arthritis, disorders, and anxieties, etc. They can expect God to deliver them in the same or greater manner in which He has delivered us.

Some of us have been delivered from addictions of all kinds: alcohol, drugs, pornography, etc. They can expect God to save and provide salvation in the same and or greater manner in which He has saved us. The greatest person that God has saved and is saving me from is myself. Sometimes I am my greatest enemy. It all stems from one aspect, **Philippians 2:5 (KJV)** 5 Let this mind be in you, which was also in Christ Jesus. Sometimes, I simply have not allowed God to renew and or transform my mind in certain areas of my thinking and or life.

It is easy for me to have His mind when the areas are submitted to Him. For instance, I have said, "Lord you can make all the decisions about my career, worship, and the place where you want me to reside. However, Lord, I want to make the decision about my mate." The area which is not submitted is the area in which my mind has not been transformed into the mind of Christ. I have given God little or no authority to impact the place of non-submission with His power, guidance, and life (breath).

Questions

    What areas of your life do you know are fully submitted to God?

___

    What areas of your life do you know have not been submitted to God?

___

    What keeps you from submitting those areas to Him (examples: fear, false sense of control, etc.)?

___

Prayer:

    Lord, we thank You for being gracious and faithful to complete the work that You have begun in us **Philippians 1:6 (NIV)**. Lord, I pray that You amplify our trust in the areas that have not been fully submitted to You. Lord, release Your grace and release us from fear in the name of Jesus. Amen. Feel free to add to this prayer point:

___

Notes & Overall Discoveries:

Chapter 33: Looking Back & Treasures in Heaven

Genesis 19:26 (AMPC): But [Lot's] wife looked back from behind him, and she became a pillar of salt.

Luke 12: 33-34 (AMPC): Sell what you possess and give donations to the poor; provide yourselves with purses and handbags that do not grow old, an unfailing and inexhaustible treasure in the heavens, where no thief comes near and no moth destroys. 34 For where your treasure is, there will your heart be also.

Matthew 6: 19-21 (AMPC): Do not gather and heap up and store up for yourselves treasures on earth, where moth and rust and worm consume and destroy, and where thieves break through and steal. 20 But gather and heap up and store for yourselves treasures in heaven, where neither moth nor rust nor worm consume and destroy, and where thieves do not break through and steal; 21 For where your treasure is, there will your heart be also.

We look towards the places, things, or people that or who have captured our hearts. We seek those treasures out as if an internal map has been placed within us. When we find that treasure, X marks the spot. Sometimes, it takes an act of God to uproot us from the place physically. However, if we never allow Him to replace the map in our hearts, we are still (emotionally, mentally, or spiritually) stuck in those places like pillars of salt. We have memorialized a good time, a good feeling, things, relationships, opportunities, and dreams gone by. We sacrifice the life of today for the yesteryear. In sacrificing our today(s) for yesterday(s), we never move into that place of promise, purpose, security, and hope for what lies ahead in our tomorrows.

Questions:

How can we allow God to replace our maps?

_____
_____
_____
_____

Can pillars of salt every become people again? If so, what is the process?

_____
_____
_____
_____

I totally believe that pillars of salt can become people again, but in that we go through dry and sometimes dead periods in our lives. All it takes to be reactivated into purpose is for us to allow God to breathe on us. All it takes is for us to let go of the dead things and move into a place of life and restoration. One step of obedience, one act of faith, can allow God to start the fire again in our hearts. That fire is an indication that we have exchanged maps; and now our treasure is the one that has captured our heart, Christ. We seek and pursue Him as if our lives depend on apprehending what has already apprehended us. **Philippians 3:12** **(AMPC)** Not that I have now attained [this ideal], or have already been made perfect, but I press on to lay hold of (grasp) and make my own, that for which Christ Jesus (the Messiah) has laid hold of me and made me His own. Some time ago I wrote a poem that encapsulates the thoughts of having God replace my map:

Grave Robbers

Lord help me to let go of all things dead

dead relationships

dead hopes

dead dreams

like winter grips and chills the earth

so, the hand of the past grasp for my hand

I'm letting go

in the hopes of Spring

I'm letting go

so that I can bloom

I'm letting go

so that I can live

Questions:

What dead things do you need to release? It is hard to let go of dead hopes when you THINK that is all you have. How can we exchange dead hopes for the expected hope and future that God has for us **Jeremiah 29: 11 (NIV)**?

_____
_____
_____
_____

What are some "Spring" hopes that you are anticipating?

_____
_____
_____
_____

Prayer:

Lord, thank You for releasing us from the dead things that do not bring life and also for breathing on the dead things that You want to live. Much like Spring, let us bloom again. Let us hope again, and let us believe again, so that we can contend for Your promises in Jesus' name, amen. Feel free to add to this prayer point:

_____
_____
_____
_____

Notes & Overall Discoveries:

Chapter 34: God's Continued Protection

Genesis 19: 29 **(AMPC):** When God ravaged and destroyed the cities of the plain [of Siddim], He [earnestly] remembered Abraham [imprinted and fixed him indelibly on His mind], and He sent Lot out of the midst of the overthrow when He overthrew the cities where Lot lived.

More often than not, we go through horrendous situations. During those times of adversity we often ask: Where is God? Does He see, and does He even care? These are the anguish cries that some have or will cry out. God is so compassionate and is for His children, during those times we need to remind ourselves in the words of Israel Houghton, "He knows our names, He knows our every thought, He sees each tear that falls and He hears us when we call" (Houghton, Lindsey, & Walker, 2005). For the God of the universe to have us (individually) fixed upon His mind is an unfathomable thought **Psalms 8:4-8** **(NIV).** We sometimes cannot focus on the few things and people under our preview. However, God has the whole world on His mind, a whole world as in He knows what Susan Thunderman of 9230 Oak Lane Street is thinking and or going through at 12:59pm (when she was five years old). Sometimes, we affix God and His activities in a fashion that make Him either too big or too small to handle our problems. In light of the fact that He created everything, this is very laughable, but nevertheless a real emotion and tactic from the enemy to make us believe that we are alone. We must safeguard our theology and break it down in simple terms "God good" and "devil bad." Thus, we can remind ourselves that the things of God are those things which edify, strengthen, draw us closer to Him while yet preserving us in His continued protection. Those things which destroy our ability to connect to God and people, kill our hope, and steal our futures are from the enemy. We must continually remind ourselves that EVERYTHING that is a concern to us is a concern to our Father. **Psalms 138: 8 (AMPC).** The Lord will perfect that which concerns me; Your mercy and loving-kindness, O Lord, endure forever—forsake not the works of Your own hands.

Questions:

> What have you been through that made you feel alone (that you did not sense the presence of God)? What truth has God revealed concerning this situation? How has he sought to free and heal you?
>
> _____
> _____
> _____
>
> Did you later see God's activity when you were no longer in the situation?
>
> _____
> _____
> _____
>
> How can you simplify your theology to hold on to the fact that God is for you, and you have an adversary (the devil)?
>
> _____
> _____
> _____
>
> What are some principles and some of God's promises that you can stand on when going through adversity?
>
> _____
> _____
> _____

Often when I have had a really trying situation, God reminds me of His promises to me, and sometimes I must remind myself (not yet, God's not done).

Prayer:

> Lord, teach us the work that You have for us (submission) and the understanding that everything else is under Your purview. Let us simplify our theology: God is good, and I have an enemy. I have an enemy that God has

already defeated and has given me the power to defeat **Luke 10:19** **(NIV)**. Lord, remove the blindness and fear that says that we are powerless **Philippians 4:13** **(NIV)**. Feel free to add to this prayer point:

_____
_____
_____
_____

Notes & Overall Discoveries:

Chapter 35: Intercession, Protection & Integrity

Author's Note: Day nine –8/8/15 – Special time in the writing process: This is the first day of filling after a long emptying process. This day is one of the first times when I really felt the wind and breath of God on the process itself and the writing. Up until this point I was writing out of obedience to God and starting with the blueprint He gave me; however, this day was a day of breakthrough. God has blessed me with a set aside time and place where He made my dead bones live, I wanted to work on a vision board, and I asked what He wanted me to do. He said…write. Thus, from this point onward the writings are more about the movement of God and my stance of obedience.

Genesis 20:1-7 (AMPC): Now Abraham journeyed from there toward the South country (the Negeb) and dwelt between Kadesh and Shur; and he lived temporarily in Gerar.2 And Abraham said of Sarah his wife, She is my sister. And Abimelech king of Gerar sent and took Sarah [into his harem].3 But God came to Abimelech in a dream by night and said, Behold, you are a dead man because of the woman whom you have taken [as your own], for she is a man's wife.4 But Abimelech had not come near her, so he said, Lord, will you slay a people who are just and innocent?5 Did not the man tell me, She is my sister? And she herself said, He is my brother. In integrity of heart and innocence of hands I have done this.6 Then God said to him in the dream, Yes, I know you did this in the integrity of your heart, for it was I Who kept you back and spared you from sinning against Me; therefore I did not give you occasion to touch her. 7 So now restore to the man his wife, for he is a prophet, and he will pray for you and you will live. But if you do not restore her [to him], know that you shall surely die, you and all who are yours.

The Lord Himself protected Abimelech from sinning against and corrupting the promise and intent to make Abraham a nation through Sarah. But God's protection was a result of innocence, integrity, and obedience. Once Abimelech knew what God did not want him to do, he obeyed God and did not do those things. However, it is human nature (sin nature) that if something is forbidden that thing becomes the most enticing thing to us until we have succumbed or resisted sin.

Genesis 2:17 (AMPC): The LORD God commanded the man, saying, "From any tree of the garden you may eat freely; 17but from the tree of the knowledge of good and evil you shall not eat, for in the day that you eat from it you will surely die."

Genesis 3: 1-6 (AMPC): Now the serpent was more subtle and crafty than any living creature of the field which the Lord God had made. And he [Satan] said to the woman, Can it really be that God has said, You shall not eat from every tree of the garden? 2 And the woman said to the serpent, We may eat the fruit from the trees of the garden,3 Except the fruit from the tree which is in the middle of the garden. God has said, You shall not eat of it, neither shall you touch it, lest you die.4 But the serpent said to the woman, You shall not surely die,5 For God knows that in the day you eat of it your eyes will be opened, and you will be like God, knowing the difference between good and evil and blessing and calamity. 6 And when the woman saw that the tree was good (suitable, pleasant) for food and that it was delightful to look at, and a tree to be desired in order to make one wise, she took of its fruit and ate; and she gave some also to her husband, and he ate.

Eating of the forbidden gives us more than just a stomachache; it causes death. Sometimes the death could be spiritually and affect our walk of obedience and our sweet communion with God. Sometimes the death could be physical as promised to Abimelech should he have touched Sarah (forbidden). He and his entire household were slated for death.

Questions:

What has God forbidden you to partake of? What protection is in that forbiddance?

_____
_____
_____
_____

For example, God has challenged me to lessen my consumption of sugar. The protections within this request are numerous: health, weight, etc. He issued this challenge by showing me the obedience of the Rechabites. **Jeremiah 35:1-16 (NIV):** The word which came to Jeremiah from the Lord in the days of Jehoiakim the son of Josiah, king of Judah, saying, 2 "Go to the house of the Rechabites, speak to them, and bring them into the house of the Lord, into one of the chambers, and give them wine to drink." 3 Then I took Jaazaniah the son of Jeremiah, the son of Habazziniah, his brothers and all his sons, and the whole house of the Rechabites, 4 and I brought them into the house of the Lord, into the chamber of the sons of Hanan the son of Igdaliah, a man of God, which was by the chamber of the princes, above the chamber of Maaseiah the son of Shallum, the keeper of the door. 5 Then I set before the sons of the house of the Rechabites bowls full of wine, and cups; and I said to them, "Drink wine." 6 But they said, "We will drink no wine, for Jonadab the son of Rechab, our father, commanded us, saying, 'You shall drink no wine, you nor your sons, forever. 7 You shall not build a house, sow seed, plant a vineyard, nor have any of these; but all your days you shall dwell in tents, that you may live many days in the land where you are sojourners.' 8 Thus we have obeyed the voice of Jonadab the son of Rechab, our father, in all that he charged us, to drink no wine all our days, we, our wives, our sons, or our daughters, 9 nor to build ourselves houses to dwell in; nor do we have vineyard, field, or seed.10 But we have dwelt in tents, and have obeyed and done according to all that Jonadab our father commanded us. 11 But it came to pass, when Nebuchadnezzar king of Babylon came up into the land, that we said, 'Come, let us go to Jerusalem for fear of the army of the Chaldeans and for fear of the army of the Syrians.' So we dwell at Jerusalem." 12 Then came the word of the Lord to Jeremiah, saying, 13 "Thus says the Lord of hosts, the God of Israel: 'Go and tell the men of Judah and the inhabitants of Jerusalem, "Will you not receive instruction to obey My words?" says the Lord. 14 "The words of Jonadab the son of Rechab, which he commanded his sons, not to drink wine, are performed; for to this day they drink none, and obey their father's commandment. But although I have spoken to you, rising early and speaking, you did not obey Me. 15 I have also sent to you all My servants the prophets, rising up early and sending them, saying, 'Turn now everyone from his evil way, amend your doings, and do not go after other gods to serve them; then you will dwell in the land which I have given you and your fathers.' But you have not inclined your ear, nor obeyed Me. 16 Surely the sons of Jonadab the son of Rechab have performed the commandment of their father, which he commanded them, but this people has not obeyed Me.

God told me that sugar was my wine. This is my forbidden, and I have gone to extremes in both ways; however, I failed to realize that I only need to heed the voice of God and be obedient. He will bring balance and alignment to my appetites.

Question:

What is your wine i.e., what is the thing that God has forbidden? How can you be intentional to obey all that God says?

_____

_____

_____

_____

Prayer:

Lord, I pray that You reveal the forbidden, so that we can hide in Your protection. Lord, let us cry out to You for strength as You provide a way of escape. **I Corinthians 10:13** **(NIV)**. Give us ways to move beyond. Give us support and accountability in Jesus' name, amen. Feel free to add to this prayer point:

_____

_____

_____

_____

Notes & Overall Discoveries:

Chapter 36: Blessings in Obedience

Genesis 20:14-18 (AMPC): Then Abimelech took sheep and oxen and male and female slaves and gave them to Abraham and restored to him Sarah his wife. 15 And Abimelech said, Behold, my land is before you; dwell wherever it pleases you. 16 And to Sarah he said, Behold, I have given this brother of yours a thousand pieces of silver; see, it is to compensate you [for all that has occurred] and to vindicate your honor before all who are with you; before all men you are cleared and compensated. So, Abraham prayed to God, and God healed Abimelech and his wife and his female slaves, and they bore children,18 For the Lord had closed fast the wombs of all in Abimelech's household because of Sarah, Abraham's wife.

Abimelech's obedience to God's command saved lives. God heard the prayers of Abraham and healed and blessed Abimelech's household with heirs. Death would have come from disobedience, but life and life more abundantly came from obedience. **John 10:10 (KJV):** The thief does not come except to steal, and to kill, and to destroy. I have come that they may have life, and that they may have it more abundantly. Abimelech's entire household, both his wife and slaves, had children. The irony is that Abraham was praying for the blessing, the miracle, and the promise (that he had yet to receive) for someone else.

Questions:

Can you pray that others receive the promise you are waiting to receive? Be it a new house, new car, education, husband, wife, or child? Can you pray in light of not seeing the fulfillment of the promise in your own life?

_____
_____
_____
_____

What keeps your heart clear from jealousy, envy, or doubt?

_____
_____
_____
_____

Can you rely on the Promise Giver's character to do just what He promised that He would do for you and others?

_____
_____
_____
_____

Do you think that your ability to pray for someone else's promise may have some attachment in releasing your own blessing?

_____
_____
_____
_____

Once God told me that intercession and worship were my warfare for deliverance. God utilized two lines in Job to showcase the power of intercession. **Job 42: 10 (AMPC):** After Job had **prayed** for his friends, the LORD restored his fortunes and gave him twice as much as he had before. The most powerful aspect of praying for someone else is for that brief moment you are not concerned for yourself. This avenue of selflessness allows God to be God in both situations; He moves on the behalf of the praying and prayed for. **Intercession is warfare** -- the key to God's battle plan for our lives. But the battleground is not of this earth. The Bible says, "We are not fighting against humans. We are fighting against forces and authorities and against rulers of darkness and spiritual powers in the heavens above" **Ephesians. 6:12 (NIV)**. The Bible has many illustrations of worship as a weapon (Jericho). Another illustration comes from **II Chronicles 20:22** (NKJV) Now when they began to sing and to praise, the Lord set ambushes against the people of Ammon, Moab, and Mount Seir, who had come against Judah; and they were defeated.

Questions:

What weapons has God given you with which to fight the enemy? Are praise and intercession among them?

_____
_____

How do you cultivate and use your weapon?

How have you seen God use your weapons?

What are your testimonies of victory? **Revelation 12:11 (NIV)** And they overcame him by the blood of the Lamb, and by the word of their testimony; and they loved not their lives unto the death.

Prayer:

Lord, we thank You that You are our victory, You help us overcome. Lord, You pray and fight for us **Romans 8: 26-27** **(NIV)**. Please let us follow Your instruction for warfare, so that we can see and experience the VICTORY in Jesus' name, amen. Feel free to add to this prayer point:

Chapter 37: Getting Rid of the Counterfeits (Inferior Promises)

<u>God Honors the Seed Promise</u>

Genesis 21:8-13: And the child grew and was weaned, and Abraham made a great feast the same day that Isaac was weaned. 9 Now Sarah saw the son of Hagar the Egyptian, whom she had borne to Abraham, mocking [Isaac]. 10 Therefore she said to Abraham, cast out this bondwoman and her son, for the son of this bondwoman shall not be an heir with my son Isaac. 11 And the thing was very grievous (serious, evil) in Abraham's sight on account of his son [Ishmael]. 12 God said to Abraham, do not let it seem grievous and evil to you because of the youth and your bondwoman; in all that Sarah has said to you, do what she asks, for in Isaac shall your posterity be called. 13 And I will make a nation of the son of the bondwoman also, because he is your offspring

The counterfeit (substitutions) cannot dwell with the superior promise. Thus, God said that Abraham should cast off Hagar and Ishmael. However, God cares about what we care about (**Psalms 138:8 NIV**) and will bless the counterfeits because of the original promise. Abraham was grieved because he was casting off his seed; but God told him not to worry because He was also going to make Ishmael a nation.

Question:

    Has God exposed a counterfeit in your life? (Example: job instead of God as the source).

_____

_____

_____

_____

In my life God has identified jobs as counterfeits in my life in that I try to "get my identity" from what I do and not who God is calling me to "be." Thus, work is ingrained and a part of me, just as Ishmael is a part of Abraham.

Questions:

    What part of you is God asking you to cast away?

_____

_____

Who is your Sarai or Sarah, your champion that is telling you to let go - to cast away? How has God stepped into that conversation to confirm His desires for you?

In the conversation that Abraham had with God, I believe that God's directives gave Abraham some peace that God would take care of Hagar and Ishmael with the promise of princes, symbolizing that Ishmael would live and prosper. What gives you peace about your act of obedience in casting away?

Prayer:

Lord, please give us strength to cast away those things that You have asked us to, if the casting away includes people, give us the promise like Ishmael that You will protect and love them. Give us the way in which to "cast away." Let us not do this out of fear or haste. Let us give grace as You direct in Jesus' name, amen. Feel free to add to this prayer point:

Chapter 38: The Weight and Cost to Carry Counterfeits

Genesis 21:14-15 (AMPC): So, Abraham rose early in the morning and took bread and a bottle of water and gave them to Hagar, putting them on her shoulders, and he sent her and the youth away. And she wandered on [aimlessly] and lost her way in the wilderness of Beersheba.

The chase or settling for the substitutes or counterfeits will have us wondering as we wander (Niles, 1933). Counterfeits weigh us down with disillusionment or discontentment because we are unfulfilled in the face of the true obtainment of the promise. The Hagar(s) and Ishmael(s) will have to be taken care of as long as they are in your camp or midst. You will have to feed them daily, and this will take away from provisions for the promise.

Questions:

What do you believe to be some counterfeits in your life? The counterfeits includes soul issues: unforgiveness, bitterness, false sense of control etc.

_____
_____
_____
_____

What are the resources being utilized to serve the counterfeits?

_____
_____
_____
_____

Prayer:

Lord, we will no longer wonder in the spirit of disillusion. We will no longer give resources (our time, money, affection) to counterfeits. We will invest in the authentic promises. We will pursue the authentic promise in Jesus' name, amen. Feel free to add to this prayer point:

_____
_____

Chapter 39: Mourning of the Perceived Death of the Promise

Genesis 21:15-16 (AMPC): 15 When the water in the bottle was all gone, Hagar caused the youth to lie down under one of the shrubs. 16 Then she went and sat down opposite him a good way off, about a bowshot, for she said, let me not see the death of the lad. And as she sat down opposite him, he lifted up his voice and wept and she raised her voice and wept.

Sometimes, distractions or counterfeits keep us from seeing that we are in mourning of the perceived death of the promise. Hagar did not want to see her promise die, so she set it down and walked away from it. When we are in a state of mourning, our vision becomes blurry or clouded by tears of anguish, disappointment, confusion: why and how are we so far away from the promise. The self-doubt and other emotions on stances could possibly include hatred (others, self, or God). The blame is a detour that I have taken that has kept me away from the promise. The sounds of wailing can be deafening and block our ability to hear instructions that will provide direction and hope.

Questions:

What have you sat down and walked away from?

_____
_____
_____
_____

What promises have you been mourning because they seem so impossible or so far out of your reach?

_____
_____
_____
_____

Is your vision blurry? Are you still on the original plan or have you detoured? God can redeem a detour (Example: Abraham and Sarah trip to Egypt)

_____
_____

How is your hearing? Can you still hear instructions that leads you out of this place of wilderness? Or are you in a place of hopelessness? How can you attune your ear to hear? (Example: worship, prayer, solitude, fasting, etc.).

Has isolation impacted your ability to hear from God? With whom do you need to be in fellowship? As we know that the enemy uses isolation as a tool against us.

What keeps you in isolation? How can you seek Godly counsel in the midst of painful (possibly shameful) situations? **Proverbs 19:20 (KJV):** Hear counsel, and receive instruction, that thou mayest be wise in thy latter end.

Prayer:

Lord, we ask that You give us instruction on how to "put our hands on the promise." Lord, please shake us out of disillusionment, disappointment, and hopelessness. Lord, give us the spirit of obedience where we can follow the path to hear again, be it fasting, prayer, worshiping, etc. We blessed You, Lord the Promise Giver and Keeper. Revive us again in Jesus' name, amen.

Chapter 40: But God Hears

Genesis 21:17 (AMPC): And God heard the voice of the youth, and the angel of God called to Hagar out of heaven and said to her, what troubles you, Hagar? Fear not, for God has heard the voice of the youth where he is.

Question:

> Why was God moved by the voice of the child possibly more than the weeping of Hagar?

_____

_____

_____

_____

God is a compassionate God; however, God was and currently is not as moved by the anguish cry as He is moved by the cries of, for, and from the seeds of promises. God hears the cries from, of, and for the seeds of promise no matter where they are in their development: intimacy, conception, labor, or delivery.

- Intimacy or foreplay – toying around with an idea or a thought
- Conception – the idea and or thought receiving the breath of life and moving into their developmental stage.
- Gestation – the growth and maturity of the idea
- Labor – the work, pain, and or pressure needed to get the idea to the delivery stage
- Delivery – carrying the promise to full term, not aborting or miscarrying the promise during the previous developmental stages.

Each stage takes obedience and a willingness to be inconvenienced, stretched to something unrecognizable, endure pain, and or suffering in light of what will manifest. The inconvenience may include the need to be prodded and examined over and over again by everyone from the person on the street to the experts in white coats. Everyone is waiting for delivery. Please know that it is not enough to say that we have been impregnated with the seed of promise from God but everyone NEEDS to see a birth to promise and not a birth to wind.

Questions:

What are you carrying?

_____
_____
_____
_____

What stage of development are you in for one specific SOPs (intimacy, conception, gestation, labor, delivery)?

_____
_____
_____
_____

What are you doing to safeguard this SOP?

_____
_____
_____
_____

Do you feel as if you have aborted or miscarried the SOP? If so, what has God said that will resuscitate and bring it back from death's grip?

_____
_____
_____
_____

Prayer:

Lord, thank You for hearing the cries from Your seeds of promise. Lord, we are Your SOPs. Let us fully grasp that you HEAR us. You hear us! When the enemy sends the lies that You are not present, silence him in Jesus' name, amen. Feel free to add to this prayer point:

_____
_____
_____

Conclusion of Part 1

This concludes Part 1 of the Guardians of Promise Book 1: Birthing the Promise. Part 2 will contain more on the following phases: gestation, labor, and delivery of the promise. I really appreciate you taking this journey with me to explore the parallel experience of natural conception and promise conception. As we are reflecting on the character of the Promise Giver and Keeper and our posture of obedience to steward the promises well, I pray that we are being transformed and see ourselves as God's seeds of promise. I cannot wait for us to give birth. See you in Part 2.

Reflections on Part 1

What aspects of promise conception are the most rewarding and most challenging to you?

Who are you giving birth with (family or community) and for (sphere of influence – you are called to champion this group of people)? The groups can be the same?

What name is Your Father calling you, and how are you mindful to answer only to the name He calls you?

What promise were you in mourning of, and how has God resurrected it?

Are you stewarding your SOPs well? If not, where can you get support and assistance?

REFERENCES

Complete List for Part 1 & Part 2

Carter, T. (1988). *Spurgeon At His Best.* Grand Rapids, MI: Baker Book House, 1991 reprinted edition, first published 1988. Pg. 67.

CBN.com. (2015). *What is intercession?* Retrieved on October 1, 2015 from http://www.cbn.com/spirituallife/cbnteachingsheets/keys-Intercession.aspx.

Circumcision (2015). HealtyChildren.org. Adapted from Caring for Your Baby and Young Child: Birth to Age Five (Copyright © 2009 American Academy of Pediatrics) Retrieved on September 18, 2015 from: https://www.healthychildren.org/English/ages-stages/prenatal/decisions-to-make/Pages/Should-the-Baby-be-Circumcised.aspx

Darwin, C. (1859). "On the Origin of Species by Means of Natural Selection, or the Preservation of Favoured Races in the Struggle for Life," p. 162. - See more at: http://www.darwins-theory-of-evolution.com/#sthash.RsM8hIIy.dpuf

Diamond, D. (2015). Scott & Diana Cody's Southland Home group. September 23, 2015.

Department of Justice. (2015). Federal *Protections Against National Origin Discrimination.* Retrieved on September 21, 2015 from: http://www.justice.gov/crt/federal-protections-against-national-origin-discrimination-1#emp.

Dove Real Beauty Sketch: You Are More Beautiful Than You Think. (April 14. 2013). Accessed on April 9, 2015 from: https://youtu.be/litXW91UauE.

Duewel, W. (1986). *Touch the world through prayer.* Grand Rapids, Mich.: F. Asbury Press.

Goll, J., & Goll, M. (2006). *Dream Language.* Shippensburg, PA: Destiny Image.

Henry, M. (1706). Bible Commentary - Matthew Henry Concise. Retrieved September 23, 2015 from http://www.biblestudytools.com/commentaries/matthew-henry-concise/.

Houghton, I, Lindsey, A. Walker. A. (2005). Alive in South Africa Disc I: *He Knows My Name*. Artists & Composers: Israel & Newbreed. Israel Houghton, Aaron Lindsey, and Tommy Walker, Released on Integrity Music.

Jack, J. (2015). Scott & Diana Cody's Southland Home group. September 23, 2015.

Johnson, B. (2008). Jesus Culture: Dallas 2008: "Heal the Sick, Raiser the Dead, Cleanse the Lepers." Retrieved on September 28, 2015 from https://www.youtube.com/watch?v=ItLIUWPujg8.

Johnson, B. (2011). What is the Spirit of Prophecy? YouTube: originally published August 8, 2011. Retrieved on September 28, 2015 from: https://youtu.be/T-6DPHmzzkc

Khan Academy. (2021). Human emryogenesis. Retrieved on September 15, 2021 from https://www.khanacademy.org/test-prep/mcat/cells/embryology/a/human-embryogenesis.

Krell, K. (2006, November 14). 22. "A Divine Encounter" (Genesis 18:1-15). Retrieved September 23, 2015 from https://bible.org/seriespage/22-divine-encounter-genesis-181-15.

L'Engle, M. (2007). *A wind in the door*. New York: Farrar, Straus and Giroux.

Navigators. (2021). *Praying the names and attributes of God: A free 30-day prayer guide*. Retrieved on August 31, 2021 from https://www.navigators.org/namesofgod.

Newton, T. (2011). TedTalk: Embracing otherness, embracing myself. Retrieved on April 9, 2015 from https://youtu.be/uzKBGtf0i0M

Niles, J. (1933). *I Wonder as I Wander*. John Jacob Niles: The Songs of John Jacob Niles. Published by G. Schirmer (HL.50481076). Retrieved on October 2, 2015 from http://www.john-jacob-niles.com/

Simon S. (2005). Big Bang: The Origin of the Universe. Harper Perennial. p. 560.

Young, D. (2015). "If there is one righteous man." Southland Church. September 2015, Valdosta Georgia.

Vallotton, K., & Johnson, B. (2006). The Supernatural Ways of Royalty: Discovering Your Rights and Privileges of Being a Son or Daughter of God. Shippenberg, PA: Destiny Image.

Wilkerson, C. (2015). "God will hide you but will not hide stuff from you."

Wine press. (nd). Retrieved from https://en.wikipedia.org/wiki/Wine_press.

ABOUT THE AUTHOR

Njeri Pringle is a three-time graduate of Valdosta State University. She is both a teacher and a life-long learner. More importantly, she is a pursuer of the Promise Giver. God captured her heart at an early age. He gave her several mandates. The Guardians of Promise is one, as well as teaching fearlessness. She has much to learn, much to do, and much to be, as being God's child is where all of her future work will flow. Look for more of the Guardians series, as God's promises are assured as Yes and Amen **(II Corinthians 1:20 NIV)**.

www.ingramcontent.com/pod-product-compliance
Lightning Source LLC
Chambersburg PA
CBHW081458040426
42446CB00016B/3304